Human Medical Trials

Other books in the At Issue in History series:

Human Medical Trials

Kelly Barth, *Book Editor*

Bruce Glassman, *Vice President*
Bonnie Szumski, *Publisher*
Helen Cothran, *Managing Editor*
Scott Barbour, *Series Editor*

 **OPPOSING VIEWPOINTS® SERIES** **AT ISSUE IN HISTORY**

GREENHAVEN PRESS
An imprint of Thomson Gale, a part of The Thomson Corporation

 THOMSON

GALE

Detroit • New York • San Francisco • San Diego • New Haven, Conn.
Waterville, Maine • London • Munich

© 2005 Thomson Gale, a part of The Thomson Corporation.

Thomson and Star Logo are trademarks and Gale and Greenhaven Press are registered trademarks used herein under license.

For more information, contact
Greenhaven Press
27500 Drake Rd.
Farmington Hills, MI 48331-3535
Or you can visit our Internet site at http://www.gale.com

Cover credit: © CORBIS/Sygma. Researchers examine anonymous participants in the Tuskegee syphilis study.

LIBRARY OF CONGRESS CATALOGING-IN-PUBLICATION DATA

Human medical trials / Kelly Barth, book editor.
    p. cm. — (At issue in history)
Includes bibliographical references and index.
ISBN 0-7377-2669-5 (lib. : alk. paper)
    1. Clinical trials—History. 2. Human experimentation in medicine—History.
3. Medicine—Research—History. I. Barth, Kelly. II. Series.
R853.C55H86 2005
610'.72—dc22   2004060744

Printed in the United States of America

Contents

was so driven to find a vaccine for hepatitis that he intentionally infected children with the virus so that he could study the progression of the disease.

Chapter 3: The Fernald School Radiation Experiments

Foreword

Historian Robert Weiss defines history simply as "a record and interpretation of past events." Both elements—record and interpretation—are necessary, Weiss argues.

> Names, dates, places, and events are the essence of history. But historical writing is not a compendium of facts. It consists of facts placed in a sequence to tell a connected story. A work of history is not merely a story, however. It also must analyze what happened and *why*—that is, it must interpret the past for the reader.

For example, the events of December 7, 1941, that led President Franklin D. Roosevelt to call it "a date which will live in infamy" are fairly well known and straightforward. A force of Japanese planes and submarines launched a torpedo and bombing attack on American military targets in Pearl Harbor, Hawaii. The surprise assault sank five battleships, disabled or sank fourteen additional ships, and left almost twenty-four hundred American soldiers and sailors dead. On the following day, the United States formally entered World War II when Congress declared war on Japan.

These facts and consequences were almost immediately communicated to the American people who heard reports about Pearl Harbor and President Roosevelt's response on the radio. All realized that this was an important and pivotal event in American and world history. Yet the news from Pearl Harbor raised many unanswered questions. Why did Japan decide to launch such an offensive? Why were the attackers so successful in catching America by surprise? What did the attack reveal about the two nations, their people, and their leadership? What were its causes, and what were its effects? Political leaders, academic historians, and students look to learn the basic facts of historical events and to read the intepretations of these events by many different sources, both primary and secondary, in order to develop a more complete picture of the event in a historical context.

In the case of Pearl Harbor, several important questions surrounding the event remain in dispute, most notably the role of President Roosevelt. Some historians have blamed his policies for deliberately provoking Japan to attack in order to propel America into World War II; a few have gone so far as to accuse him of knowing of the impending attack but not informing others. Other historians, examining the same event, have exonerated the president of such charges, arguing that the historical evidence does not support such a theory.

The Greenhaven At Issue in History series recognizes that many important historical events have been interpreted differently and in some cases remain shrouded in controversy. Each volume features a collection of articles that focus on a topic that has sparked controversy among eyewitnesses, contemporary observers, and historians. An introductory essay sets the stage for each topic by presenting background and context. Several chapters then examine different facets of the subject at hand with readings chosen for their diversity of opinion. Each selection is preceded by a summary of the author's main points and conclusions. A bibliography is included for those students interested in pursuing further research. An annotated table of contents and thorough index help readers to quickly locate material of interest. Taken together, the contents of each of the volumes in the Greenhaven At Issue in History series will help students become more discriminating and thoughtful readers of history.

Introduction

Since the middle of the twentieth century, Americans have become deeply concerned about human medical trials, experiments conducted on people for the purpose of scientific discovery or medical advancement. This concern arose in large part because of the post–World War II revelation of the cruel and often fatal medical experiments conducted primarily on Jewish people in the Nazi concentration camps. In fact, so strong was the conviction that no such experiments should ever again take place that the American medical community participated in the writing of an international document, the Nuremberg Code, a universal code of medical ethics that contains regulations governing medical experiments.

Among the many reasons people were so outraged by the Nazi experiments was that the researchers had rationalized them by performing them on what they believed was a dispensable population of humans. Three now infamous twentieth-century American medical experiments have drawn similar condemnation: the Tuskegee syphilis study, the Willowbrook school hepatitis study, and the Fernald school radiation study. In all three cases the experiments were conducted on an especially vulnerable population poorly equipped to question the experiments or defend themselves from manipulation or harm. The Tuskegee syphilis study, which began in the 1930s, was conducted on poor, uneducated African American men. Both the Willowbrook school and Fernald school studies were performed on institutionalized children, many of whom were mentally retarded.

The Tuskegee Syphilis Study

When the Tuskegee study began in 1932, syphilis, a debilitating and, if left untreated, fatal sexually transmitted disease, had already reached epidemic proportions in many areas of the United States. However, researchers from the U.S. Public Health Service (PHS) made southern blacks the focus of the study because they believed this group of people exhibited what Harvard medical historian Allan M. Brandt has called "an excessive sexual desire"[1] that left them particularly susceptible to venereal diseases. Further, researchers believed that because these men had never before been treated for the disease and were unlikely to be treated before they succumbed to it, they provided an unprecedented opportunity to observe and document the effects of syphilis on the human body.

After conducting a survey to determine which southern county had the highest population of African Americans suffering from the disease, PHS researchers recruited four hundred syphilitic black men aged twenty-five to sixty from Macon County, Alabama. They secured the participation of the local health clinic, which supplied an African American nurse, and also enlisted the help of the African American–staffed Tuskegee University Hospital in maintaining regular contact and good rapport with the participants.

Although the men were led to believe that in participating in the free study, they would be treated for syphilis or what they called "bad blood," they received virtually no treatment at all. Other than painful diagnostic procedures to confirm the continued presence of syphilis, the men received only mercury ointment treatments, which eased the disease's symptoms but not its progression. Even after a PHS discovery in the early 1940s that penicillin had a curative effect on early and even some late stages of syphilis, Tuskegee study participants were not given the antibiotic nor were they encouraged to seek treatment elsewhere. Telling the men about other treatment options would have conflicted with the researchers' ultimate goal of conducting autopsies on the participants' bodies to document the disease's various effects.

When Associated Press reporter Jean Heller wrote an exposé about the Tuskegee study in 1972, both the American public and government officials were outraged. Senator Edward Kennedy held hearings to gather facts, and in 1973 the findings were used to halt the study. Though the U.S. Centers for Disease Control did offer to locate all the participants and to pay for their continued treatment, they did not offer to compensate the men for their suffering. However, as a result of a 1974 class-action lawsuit, a settlement of $10 million was divided among the surviving Tuskegee study participants and their families. By then, 129 men had died as a result of failing to receive treatment during the study. Finally in 1997, sixty-five years after the study began, President Bill Clinton publicly apologized to study participants and their families on behalf of the nation.

The Willowbrook Hepatitis Study

Throughout the first half of the twentieth century there was no known cure for hepatitis, a highly contagious disease that attacks the liver and that is spread by the exchange of bodily fluids. Like syphilis, hepatitis was a serious public health problem, especially in institutional settings. The Willowbrook school, a home for mentally retarded children in Staten Island, New York, was one of the hardest-hit institutions. In fact, so many residents of the chronically overcrowded school were infected with the disease that new residents were virtually guaranteed to contract it within months of moving there.

Saul Krugman, the consulting physician at Willowbrook, and a staff of epidemiologists he assembled, viewed conditions at the school as the perfect opportunity to research the disease in the hope of discovering a vaccine. In 1964 they began the now infamous Willowbrook hepatitis study. Rather than conduct research on Willowbrook residents already infected with hepatitis, Krugman and his fellow researchers fed dozens of new and previously uninfected residents live hepatitis virus and then kept them in isolation from the rest of the institution's population to study the disease's progression and effects. During the study some of the participants were treated with the drug gamma globulin, which had been shown to reduce the disease's harmful effects. Many, however, were not.

Despite Krugman's noble aim of finding a cure for hepatitis, many in the medical community ultimately questioned the ethics of his research. Although it is true that participants were enrolled in the study only after their parents granted permission, the information the researchers gave to those parents was coercive and often misleading. For example, as medical ethicists David J. Rothman and Sheila M. Rothman point out in their book *The Willowbrook Wars*, though the letter given to parents "twice described introducing the live virus as a 'new form of protection,' . . . feeding a child hepatitis hardly amounted to prevention. In truth, the goal of the experiment was to create, not deliver, a new form of protection."[2] In addition, these parents, all desperate to find institutional care for their severely disabled children, were coerced into enrolling them in the program because their acceptance at overcrowded Willowbrook was contingent upon it.

Medical ethicists also questioned whether it was ever justified to intentionally infect any healthy child with a disease whether their parents had given permission or not. Though no study participants died while residents of Willowbrook, being infected with the virus left them vulnerable to more serious second attacks of the disease even though their first case may have been mild. Also, although researchers understood how hepatitis was passed from one resident to another, they did little outside their experimental ward to help the Willowbrook school institute hygiene practices that would have curbed its spread. At the completion of the experiments, all Willowbrook study participants were given therapeutic drugs for their hepatitis, but some medical ethicists argue that the children could have been protected from contracting hepatitis in the first place rather than being used in experiments designed to learn more about the disease.

Years after the Willowbrook study ended in 1976, Krugman continued to defend his research and use of child "volunteers" against an onslaught of attacks from the medical community. Although he and his fellow researchers ultimately were not the ones to discover a vaccine for the disease, they argued that their research had led, at least in part, to this discovery.

The Fernald School Radiation Experiments

In the late 1940s and early 1950s Americans understandably became fearful of the power of radiation. The dropping of the first atomic bomb during World War II had revealed its destructive potential. In response to concerns over possible nuclear attack, Americans conducted nuclear bomb tests in the deserts of the American Southwest to better understand the effects of destruction and radioactive fallout. In addition, federal agencies made hundreds of millions of dollars available to scientists to devise and conduct a myriad of experiments that would provide data about radiation's effects on humans. Some researchers even began to experiment with radioactive elements, which could be easily detected and tracked in the body and were thus attractive for use in nutrition experiments.

One such experiment took place at the Walter E. Fernald State School for mentally retarded children in Waltham, Massachusetts, a suburb of Boston. A group of boys was fed hot cereal mixed with radioactive calcium as part of an experiment to determine whether phytates, naturally occurring chemicals found in breakfast-cereal grains such as farina and oatmeal, would affect the body's ability to absorb calcium in milk. The radioactive calcium was used because it could easily be traced in stool and blood samples collected from the boys. The study was funded by the Quaker Oats Company and a government agency called the Atomic Energy Commission, and the research was conducted by a group that included doctors from the Fernald school and scientists from the Massachusetts Institute of Technology (MIT).

Aside from the obvious ethical dilemma of feeding children radioactive food, another major problem with the Fernald study was the method of participant selection. The study was presented to the more than fifty boys and their parents not as a medical experiment but as an opportunity to participate in an exclusive science club. Parents were told that if they gave their consent, their sons would receive special privileges such as parties, presents, and outings. They were also told that their sons would be participating in a nutritional study that would allow them to eat a diet especially rich in vitamins and minerals. Though both the boys and their parents were told the boys had been selected for the science club based on their superior intelligence, they were in reality chosen because they met the experiment's height, weight, and overall health requirements. The boys were told their participation in the science club experiment would result in significant benefits to people. However, neither they nor their parents were ever told that they would be ingesting radioactive food.

Deceiving the study participants was just one of many injustices they suffered as residents of the Fernald school. As was the case at many schools for the mentally disabled, conditions at the Fernald school were notoriously poor. Though many were mentally retarded, others had only mild learning disabilities. Others who were of normal intelligence were enrolled there because of behavioral problems. Because all the boys were treated as if they had the same problem, many of their unique needs went unaddressed. Worse, students were often neglected or abused. Any hope for special privileges and a break in the tedium was therefore a strong incentive for the boys to join the science club. Also, as investigative journalist Michael D'Antonio writes in his book *The State Boys Rebellion*, the status of being in the science club was the greatest reward for the boys because "it was for the smarter boys. They were proud to belong."[3]

Throughout the early 1990s journalists around the country exposed many such radiation experiments funded by the Atomic Energy Commission. The truth behind the Fernald school experiment was brought to light in 1993 when Sandra Marlow, a librarian at the school, became curious about documents she found in the archive. She began to piece together the science club story and contacted Scott Allen, a reporter with the *Boston Globe*. Allen's story about the experiments appeared in the December 26, 1993, edition of the newspaper. Throughout 1994 new revelations about the Fernald school radiation experiments appeared in the *Globe* on a nearly daily basis.

As a result of this media exposure of the experiments, the Task Force on Human Subject Research was established in 1994 by the Commonwealth of Massachusetts to look into the allegations and write its own report. Even though the consensus among the task force of politicians, doctors, ethicists, and lawyers was that the doses of radiation were small enough that they would not have caused any lasting health effects on the boys, it concluded that the deceptive and manipulative methods used to elicit the boys' participation were unethical. The task force also concluded that learning the truth about how the boys had been manipulated into becoming involved in a study that they and their parents only partially understood had caused surviving participants emotional distress.

Two events brought the now-grown participants some closure. These former members of the Fernald science club filed a class action lawsuit, and in December 1995 received a combined settlement of a little more than $3 million from Quaker Oats, MIT, the Commonwealth of Massachusetts, and the federal government. Also, in October of that same year, President Bill Clinton offered a collective apology to them and other victims of the many government-sponsored radiation experiments that had been conducted across the country.

Human medical trials have been and will continue to be a crucial tool in treating disease and improving the health of people around the world. However, strict treatment protocols must be in place to protect study participants. In addition to the Nuremberg Code, other medical ethics legislation such as the Declaration of Helsinki and the International Ethical Guidelines for Biomedical Research Involving Human Subjects, which was established by the Council for International Organizations of Medical Services, have been put into place to protect subjects. Participants must now be fully informed about an experiment and its risks. Also, institutional review boards must review an experiment before it begins and monitor both the researchers and subjects throughout the experiment. Use of preventative therapies is now mandatory as well. The legacy that survivors of the Tuskegee, Willowbrook, and Fernald studies continue to offer is the reminder that legislative vigilance is needed to prevent a repetition of their suffering.

Notes

1. Allan M. Brandt, "Racism and Research: The Case of the Tuskegee Syphilis Experiment," *Hastings Center Report*, December 1978, p. 22.
2. David J. Rothman and Sheila M. Rothman, *The Willowbrook Wars*. New York: Harper & Row, 1984, p. 266.
3. Michael D'Antonio, *The State Boys Rebellion*. New York: Simon & Schuster, 2004, p. 56.

Chapter 1

The Tuskegee Syphilis Study

1

The Tuskegee Study Will Help Stop Syphilis from Harming Everyone

Thomas Parran

In 1934, while he was surgeon general of the United States, Thomas Parran, one of the doctors involved in the Tuskegee syphilis study, wrote a book about his experiences called *Shadow on the Land: Syphilis.* In the following selection Parran describes how his team engaged participants for their study and how they treated those infected. According to Parran, the team decided to treat only those who had recently contracted the disease because these people were the most infectious. Parran then goes on to say that whites held many misconceptions about blacks that helped spread the disease. For example, many whites believed that blacks were responsible for having contracted syphilis. In fact, Parran argues, blacks owe their syphilis to the white slaveholders who infected them and their ancestors. Also, he disputes the belief commonly held by whites then that it was only blacks who were promiscuous and thus vulnerable to the disease. He warns whites that they are also vulnerable to the ravages of syphilis if the disease is allowed to spread further.

In the first place, it is true in the South, by and large, that the Negro instinctively trusts the white man, except where he has suffered from sharp dealing and has good reason to be suspicious. He trusts the doctor—thanks to the fine character of many of our rural southern physicians. He

Thomas Parran, "White Man's Burden," *Shadow on the Land: Syphilis.* New York: Reynal & Hitchcock, 1934.

trusts the Government, because in spite of clumsy dealing and mistakes since the post–civil war period, he has believed that the Government is a friend of his and tries to help him. The "government health doctor" therefore has an entrée. If he deals fairly and is considerate, it is not too difficult to get co-operation.

The Negro trusts the elders of his own race. Their older generation has an influence with the young that is far greater than among us. He trusts the educated man and woman of his race; except, again, when he has suffered from some attempt of theirs to take advantage of his lack of education. The negro preacher, the school-teacher, the occasional doctor are the acknowledged leaders of their race. Arrangements were made through them for talks in the schools and churches.

Though most of the audience did not know the word syphilis, many of them were familiar with what they called "bad-blood" disease and the miseries it brought. After the talk came the call for testing. Sometimes it was done on the spot, blood specimens taken from everybody in the place, and a date set for a second clinic to which each person present was asked to bring all members of his own family and his friends. Usually it was not difficult to get blood specimens from the whole crowd, once a leader among them had been persuaded to submit to the first test. When testing was done at a school session, a lollypop apiece helped to motivate the timid small fry.

Whites Had an Incentive to Treat Black Workers

We had some good arguments to use in conferences with the plantation owners and white leaders of the community. Public health in the South has done some impressive things in the reduction of typhoid fever, malaria, and pellagra [disease caused by niacin deficiency]. Some of the old-timers could remember the terror of yellow fever [a mosquito-borne virus] and how it had vanished. In asking help for syphilis control, I am not ashamed of the fact that we made a great point of the improved labor efficiency that would result from healthy Negroes, though I am glad to say that every doctor and nurse who worked on the project was thinking in the more human terms of relief from suffering, prevention of needless deaths, and the addition to human happiness.

After all, however, whether it is public health or sewing

machines you have to sell, you must talk to your customer in his own language. I knew that the majority of these plantation owners, fine fellows that they were, would give us their sympathetic good wishes in whatever we ourselves chose to do to improve the welfare and promote the happiness of the Negroes on their plantations. But if we expected them to do anything about it, I knew we had to use the argument that it would be more profitable to work a healthy field hand than a sick one.

I am glad to say that every doctor and nurse who worked on the project was thinking in the more human terms of relief from suffering, prevention of needless deaths, and the addition to human happiness.

Usually we got a prompt response. "Tell those niggers the health doctor will be at the Possom Hollow school tonight. He's got some government medicine to cure the blood disease. A lot of these niggers have got blood trouble, sickly, no 'count, lazy; but maybe it's not their fault. This doctor will find out." Or again, "Yes, Doc, go ahead, I've got about forty of them here pickin' cotton. Can you test them here? How long does it take?"

Man, woman, or child, as one after another reached the end of the cotton row, there was the doctor to take the blood test and a brief history. Some would hold back, only to be joshed by the more courageous fellows who had found the test not to be much of an ordeal.

Late-Stage Syphilis Not Worth Treating

We debated at length one question: Should we disregard the cases of late syphilis, concentrating on the early infectious case? Public health theory said, "Yes. The old syphilitic can't hurt anyone but himself. Concentrate on the infectious cases and try to slow up the spread." The practical psychology . . . said, "No. Treat the old syphilitic with 'rheumatism,' give him the painless mercury rubs. He will feel better and will bring in the whole family for the treatment they need. Don't forget, they listen to their granddaddies."

It was decided not to give intravenous (arsphenamine

[arsenic-based substance]) treatment to those over 50, or whose history of syphilis antedated 20 years. It was early decided, too, that intramuscular injections of bismuth or mercury in the buttocks could not be used. Except with very careful management, they may cause painful lumps which, it had been observed in clinics, the Negro particularly dislikes. How, then, could the heavy metals be given effectively?

Mercury ointment is effective if rubbed in properly. The rural Negroes wear no shoes, so ointment in the sock was out of the question. On ships in the early days it was traditional for the syphilitic sailors to sit on stools in a circle, backs bare, and rub each other with mercury ointment.

Could the same plan be used here? Get them together in the church, sitting in a circle, have the pastor lead them in a spiritual, keeping time to the up-and-down and round-and-round rubbing of mercury ointment into the backs. This was tried, but with indifferent success; partly, someone said, because the pastor thought he didn't get rubbed hard enough.

The Negro is not to blame because his syphilis rate is six times that of the white.

The best method proved to be the use of a mercury ointment on a rubber and canvas belt—endowed by the doctor, it is true, with all the white magic of health and strength-giving qualities his tongue could contrive.

"Take this package of salve, cut it into six pieces. Every morning, smear one piece on the belt; like this. Tie the belt tightly around your waist; on the seventh day, wash yourself thoroughly and meet me here. Don't forget, one week from today, and you'll feel strong as a mule."

At first, we cast about for a place where we could get such belts, cheaply, because the budget was small. There were no W.P.A. sewing rooms then. But then, as now, there was the Red Cross. In half a dozen county seats, the local chapters made the canvas and rubber belts in their sewing rooms by the hundreds, at a cost of only a few cents for the materials. . . .

Are Negros to Blame?

The Negro is not to blame because his syphilis rate is six times that of the white. He was free of it when our ancestors brought him from Africa. It is not his fault that the disease is biologically different in him than in the white; that his blood vessels are particularly susceptible so that late syphilis brings with it crippling circulatory diseases, cuts his working usefulness in half, and makes him an unemployable burden upon the community in the last years of his shortened life. It is through no fault of hers that the colored woman remains infectious two and one-half times as long as the white woman. In the white man, diseases of the central nervous system are more likely to occur; but though there are some racial differences in the type of disablement suffered by white and black in late syphilis, both pay the extreme penalty.

It has been argued that greater sexual promiscuity accounts for the increased prevalence of syphilis among the Negro. Even if this were true, and it is certainly not the whole truth, whose fault is it? Promiscuity occurs among the black race as it does among the white in groups and communities of the underprivileged. It is the smug citizen, satisfied with the *status quo*, who is to blame for the children, black or white, without moral standards, brought up in the slums, without decent education, wholesome play, or useful work, without ambition because without hope.

I cannot see how the white man may divest himself of his burden of responsibility for syphilis among the Negro by being sanctimonious about it.

We are apt to think of slums as belonging to the congested districts of the great cities. The rural slums where many Negroes live in this country are far more miserable. They are tucked away where complacent white folks are not reminded of them. They are teeming with disease. There are no school doctors to find sick children; no clinics where the sick and the handicapped receive help; no visiting nurses to look after the sick in their homes. There is no control over polluted milk or water and there is very little milk. There is no money to buy medical service, and only a little offered through charity.

In many sections of the deep South, until some very recent efforts to improve his economic status without doing much to improve the Negro to take advantage of it, the only wholesome influence the Negro has enjoyed has been the influence of his religion. And simple-minded folk, no matter what their color, would be apt to find religion more convincing if they saw more of it practiced by the white people they know who seem to have enough to eat. As it stands, the restrictions of a good life are preached to the Negro, while the rewards of a good life invariably seem to go to someone else. Even the exhortation is likely to be sporadic, for most of the great churches apparently take more real interest in saving the souls of the brown or yellow heathen in far countries than in services to the souls within our immediate boundaries.

Wherever education and living conditions among the negro race approximate that of the white race, the syphilis rate approximates that of the white. . . .

All Are Susceptible

Promiscuity, with its admitted impetus to the spread of syphilis, occurs among both white and black where we permit children to grow up ignorant among depraved surroundings. I cannot see how the white man may divest himself of his burden of responsibility for syphilis among the Negro by being sanctimonious about it.

Ignoring the psychological advantage of facing our problems squarely, however, there may be those who are comforted by feeling superior to the poor, ignorant, unmoral creatures, who fall sick and die so readily from the disease we gave them. Such superior beings need to be frightened within an inch of their lives, however, about their own lack of safety from infection if this is allowed to continue. For it is my firm belief that no man or woman, no family, can be so highly placed, so surrounded by privilege, as to be safe from syphilis if we permit it to saturate the deep strata of the less privileged, white and black, in our civilization.

2

The Tuskegee Researchers Should Be Tried in Court

James Hoge

James Hoge was just one of many newspaper editors across the United States who quickly condemned the Tuskegee study when the story broke in 1972. Since, as he notes in the following editorial, many participants actually died as a result of the "nontreatment" they received, the Department of Health, Education and Welfare had begun a formal legal investigation of the study. Hoge argues that criminal trials should be held to determine the guilt of the Tuskegee researchers. He also states that at the very least, the men and their families deserve both a public apology and monetary compensation for the pains they have suffered. In 1974 the six hundred Tuskegee victims and their families received a collective settlement of $10 million. In 1996, twenty-four years after Hoge's editorial, the victims and their families received an apology from President Bill Clinton on behalf of the U.S. government. James Hoge was an editor at the *Chicago Sun-Times*.

W hat happened to 400 black syphilitics who were heartlessly used as human guinea pigs by the United States Public Health Service at Tuskegee, Ala., during a 40-year medical experiment must be considered a crime. This dark mark on the medical profession was more than a case of bad judgment by the doctors involved. As Dr. Donald

Printz of the Center for Disease Control in Atlanta said, the study was "a literal death sentence" for some of the patients.

At this late date it may be difficult to sort out the responsibility for the mishandling of human lives.

At this late date it may be difficult to sort out the responsibility for the mishandling of human lives. Dr. John R. Heller, former government doctor who was in charge of the Tuskegee Study in 1933–34, says there was nothing in the experiment that was "unethical or unscientific." But the hard facts so far discovered appear to contradict that generalization. An effort should be made by government, medical and legal authorities to determine if there is a legal basis for bringing of criminal charges.

Treatment Was Inadequate

The experiment began in 1932. It was an inquiry into the effects of syphilis. Six hundred black men were recruited. One-third were not infected and were used as controls to judge the others. Two hundred who had the disease were not told of their condition or given treatment. The remainder were supposed to have been treated but it appears that none was.

Dr. Heller says he believed that all of the infected participants received treatment from private doctors and clinics. But he did not know how many nor were checks made to ensure that patients actually went to doctors to whom he said they were referred. Public Health Service records show none ever received treatment. In another interview, Dr. J.W. Williams, a black Tuskegee physician who worked on the experiment as an intern, said no interns had been informed of the purposes or procedures of the study.

When the experiment began, the only known treatment was arsenic and mercury, which were painful and protracted cures. But 15 years later penicillin became available. It was not administered to the subjects. Whoever made the decision to withold penicillin compounded the original immorality of the project. The subjects still alive—74—are now too old for the penicillin treatment to be useful.

At the Atlanta disease control center, it has been estimated at least seven men died directly from syphilis. The disease can lead to bone deformities, insanity, tooth decay, blindness, deafness and heart disease. And death. One subject said he had been told merely that he had "bad blood."

The subjects were persuaded to cooperate in the experiment by being given free transportation to hospitals, free hot lunches, free treatment for ailments other than syphilis and—mark this—free burial.

Were Laws Broken?

Alabama authorities are checking to see whether laws requiring mandatory treatment of venereal disease had been violated. The Department of Health, Education and Welfare has started a formal inquiry. An important first question: Do any other such experiments exist?

Besides determining culpability in this death-by-neglect experiment, the government owes the survivors and families of victims a public apology and material compensation to give substance to the apology.

3

A Physician Defends the Tuskegee Study

R.H. Kampmeier

In the following editorial for the *Southern Medical Journal*, R.H. Kampmeier, a physician and professor at Vanderbilt University's school of medicine, offered an alternative view to the numerous editorials condemning the Tuskegee syphilis study after the story broke in the early 1970s. He reviews the study's history to offer what he considers a more rational, fair, and scientific portrayal than what he perceives as hysterical and ill-informed media reports. Though he does concede that some proven antisyphilitic treatments could have been administered to and benefited the participants, he maintains that the men should have sought out and demanded those treatments from doctors who could provide them. Kampmeier advocates an unprecedented shift of the responsibility of healing from the physician to the patient. His opinions stand in stark contrast with the study's critics, who argue that because participants believed they were already being treated and because they trusted the researchers, they should not have been expected to seek alternative treatment.

The news media recently raised a great hue and cry following revelation of the study of a group of untreated syphilitics which was begun now 40 years ago and came to be known as the Tuskegee Study. Accounts and editorials in the printed news media stated outright or implied that treatment was purposefully withheld to evaluate the course of untreated disease. Only two will be quoted. *Time* stated, ". . . people

R.H. Kampmeier, "The Tuskegee Study of Untreated Syphilis," *Southern Medical Journal*, vol. 65, October 1972. Copyright © 1972 by Lippincott, Williams & Wilkins. Reproduced by permission.

with syphilis were induced to go without treatment. . . . for the past 25 years, the service has had a proven remedy available and *neglected* to use it on its select test cases. . . ." Even the *AMA* [American Medical Association] *News* was trapped into writing, "None of the men in the study received treatment for syphilis, even after the *effectiveness* of penicillin became known." (The italics are the Editor's.)

In complete disregard of their abysmal ignorance, members of the fourth estate [the press] bang out anything on their typewriters which will make headlines. Small wonder [Canadian physician] William Osler wrote more than half a century ago,

> Believe nothing that you see in the newspapers—they have done more to create dissatisfaction than all other agencies. If you see anything in them that you know is true, begin to doubt it at once.

Putting the Controversy to Rest

An exposition of the quarter-truth publicized will not reach the eyes of newsmen. It is just as well for it would be over their heads; furthermore they live to write today and to forget tomorrow, irresponsible in the "dissatisfaction" they create. Only a handful of us are left, who had much experience in the management of syphilis at about the time of the inception of the Tuskegee Study and who thus might put this recent "tempest in a teapot" into proper historical perspective. Therefore, I have elected to review the setting of the study in 1932 and its continuation as a text for the education of the younger generation of physicians, the majority of whom have little knowledge of the venereal diseases. I have reviewed the papers upon the Tuskegee Study published over three decades to refresh my memory of their content. . . .

The historical background for the Tuskegee Study begun in 1932 may be summarized as follows: (a) One study of the unmodified natural history of syphilis was extant, based on clinical diagnosis. (b) Within a half dozen years *Treponema pallidum* [organism that causes syphilis] was identified, a not highly sensitive serologic [study using blood serum] test was developed, and a treponemicidal [capable of killing *Treponema pallidum*] drug was produced. (c) After almost a decade of dependence upon a costly foreign supply of arsenicals [drugs with an arsenic base], neoarsphenamine [an early drug used to treat syphilis] became available for general use by doctors unskilled in intravenous therapy and without guidelines as to what constituted adequate treatment, hence with frequent untoward effects and with results *commonly worse than no treatment* in terms of relapse resulting from interference with the development of natural immunity. (d) Only in the year of the initiation of the Study did it become apparent as to what might constitute adequate treatment of *early* syphilis, with no inkling of the effect of arsenotherapy in later years of the disease. (e) And, finally, at that time it would have been a rare circumstance that an indigent person in a rural southern county would [have] received adequate weekly metal therapy for 60 and more weeks.

Review of the Tuskegee Study

This was conceived in 1932 following a serologic survey of 1,782 male Negroes over age 25 in Macon County in 1931–33. Among these were 472 with at least 2 positive tests and 275 who had had treatment during the first 2 years of the disease. In 1933, the initial examinations were recorded of 399 untreated Negro syphilitic men, 201 presumed non-syphilitic men, and the 275 syphilitic men who had had variable amounts of antisyphilitic treatment. "The patients who had syphilis were all in the latent [present in body, but not yet causing symptoms] stage: any acute cases requiring treatment were carefully screened out for standard therapy." The subjects thus had latent syphilis and were grouped as having become infected 3 years, 6 years, and 9 years previously—a highly significant fact (ie, syphilis of 19, 22, and 25 years' duration before the penicillin, which the news media think should have been used, became generally available). It is clear that the subjects were not deterred from obtaining treatment if they desired it or bothered to get what was available, the news media to the contrary. The report of the study at the 12 year point states that during these years a "considerable proportion of the syphilitics had received small amounts of treatment (usually 1 or 2 injections) although 12 had received as many as 10 injections." (These now needed to be excluded from the study.) The fifth paper in 1954 comments that most of the study group remained untreated although "after careful questioning, it was found that 34 of 133 patients with syphilis had received injections or oral medication which might possibly have been penicillin; 11 of the 34 received more than 5 injections." It was commented that general medical care had not improved in 20 years, and although there are excellent medical facilities in the county, costs are prohibitive or patients are unaware of them. . . .

History Sets the Record Straight

This editorial was undertaken and completed after many hours of "library research" to clarify details surrounding the Tuskegee Study. The primary purpose is to expose the deleterious ramifications of an irresponsible press in its criticisms of the ethics and actions of the medical profession in its constant age-long efforts to improve the health of the human race. Secondly, it has the purpose of emphasizing Osler's aphorism concerning the press and to put the profession always on guard in this respect and to urge disbelief of the press until proven facts appear. Thirdly, by putting the Tuskegee Study in historical perspective, hopefully the reader will have learned that syphilitic disease acquired in 1921, 1924, and 1929 would have benefited not at all from the antisyphilitic treatment as used in those days or in 1932, the time of setting the Study, in terms of the *unlikelihood* of continuous adequate therapy. Additionally, it should be clear that treatment was *not* withheld, and though no treatment was forced upon men of the Study, they had the freedom of taking what treatment they found convenient or could afford as did their brethren in the community. (That some availed themselves of this is documented, both as regards metal therapy and penicillin.). . .

Only a handful of us are left, who had much experience in the management of syphilis at about the time of the inception of the Tuskegee Study and who thus might put this . . . "tempest in a teapot" into proper historical perspective.

The implications for the Tuskegee Study are that if the men having latent syphilis of 3, 6 or 9 years' duration had been *forced* to take adequate treatment (60 or more weekly doses of a metal), cardiovascular syphilis might have been avoided in most. In our free society, antisyphilitic treatment has never been forced. Since these men did not elect to obtain treatment available to them, the development of aortic disease [a complication of syphilis] lay at the subject's door and not in the Study's protocol. As for the failure to exhibit penicillin in the treatment of these patients the same statements apply—in fact it has been indicated above that 34 patients had received treatment with penicillin. Such treatment was, of course, of little significance, since syphilis generally takes its toll in mortality and/or morbidity by a quarter of a century after infection. Obviously much literature has accumulated in the area of syphilitic cardiovascular disease since the papers quoted in the thirties and early forties. However, attention to them would be inappropriate in a discussion of continuing evaluations of the Tuskegee Study which were based on concepts of diagnosis and treatment as practiced in the days of arsenotherapy.

That some availed themselves of [alternative treatment] is documented, both as regards metal therapy and penicillin.

Though the "curative" effect of 60 injections of a metal in *continuous* order, and later a few injections of penicillin in the treatment of early syphilis became firmly established, the effectiveness of treatment of late, and especially late latent syphilis has never been so well proven. The Tuskegee Study was undertaken to shed some light on this. . . . That these questions still remain is suggested by a recommendation of the National Commission on Venereal Disease,

> That studies be undertaken to determine the effectiveness of current treatment of syphilis and gonorrhea, particularly of late latent and tertiary syphilis [the disease's third and final stage].

Treatment Would Not Have Helped

Finally, in *recapitulation*, certain facts evolve. (a) At no time in the 40 year Tuskegee Study is there a hint that treatment desired by a subject was denied him; in fact all the periodic reviews reveal that more and more of the subjects had chosen to be treated *under the same circumstances as others in their community*, albeit inadequately, but as elected by the patient and/or his doctor. (The report of 10 years stated all but one of the syphilitic group still living had had antisyphilitic treatment.) (b) The prognosis therefore in patients having late latent syphilis in the Study group was no better or no worse than that of many hundreds of thousands of other syphilitic US citizens of their generation bearing the diagnosis of late latent syphilis. (c) The most important manifestation of late syphilis, aortitis, as diagnosed in the uncomplicated state during the earlier years of the Study was *on dubious, or at best* upon controversial grounds. (d) The lethal complications of aortitis . . . had never been proven indubitably to be altered by antisyphilitic treatment. (e) Granted *adequate* treatment of late latent syphilis might have delayed or avoided the complications of aortitis, but accepting the clinical experience that these complications develop by about a quarter of a century after infection, it becomes obvious that the institution of penicillin treatment at 19, 22, and 25 years after infection would raise questions. Firstly, why should these men be singled out over their fellows in the community for treatment not forced upon others, and secondly, would it alter the prognosis at all? (f) The Study has shown that untreated syphilis is accompanied by morbidity, mortality and pathologic findings as described by others in the past.

This editorial should point up Osler's accusations directed to an irresponsible press, and the irrelevancy of certain Congressmen's emotional reaction to the Tuskegee Study.

4

Tuskegee Participants Provide Testimony

Edward Kennedy

After the press released the story of the Tuskegee syphilis study in 1972, the Senate held a hearing with some surviving participants in response to widespread concern over the study and similar human medical experiments. In the following transcript of the hearing, Massachusetts senator Edward Kennedy asks the study participants pointed questions about their experiences, in particular, whether they felt they had been misled into believing that the treatments had been conducted to heal them rather than as an experiment. In the transcript, study participants declare publicly that they suffered physical and mental pain as a result of the study. The transcripts of the Senate hearings gave the American public its first opportunity to learn what actually happened to the Tuskegee study participants.

S ENATOR [EDWARD] KENNEDY: Maybe we could talk a little bit with Mr. [Lester] Scott and Mr. [Charlie] Pollard.

Maybe both of you gentlemen would be kind enough to tell us a little bit how you were first enrolled in the study, how you heard about it, if you can remember back to those days, how you became enrolled.

Let's start with you, Mr. Pollard. Would you tell us a little bit about how you heard about this study, how you became involved?

MR. POLLARD: Back in 1932, I was going to school

Edward Kennedy, "Testimony by Four Survivors from the United States Senate Hearings on Human Experimentation, 1973," *Quality of Health Care: Human Experimentation, 1973*, hearings before the Subcommittee on Health of the Committee on Labor and Public Welfare, 93rd Congress, vol. 3. Washington, DC, 1973.

back then and they came around and said they wanted to have a clinic blood testing up there.

KENNEDY: How old were you then?

POLLARD: How old was I? Well, I was born in 1906. I had been married—no, I hadn't been married. Anyhow, they came around give us the blood tests. After they give us the blood tests, all up there in the community, they said we had bad blood. After then they started giving us the shots and give us the shots for a good long time. I don't remember how long it was. But after they got through giving us those shots, they give me a spinal tap. That was along in 1933. They taken me over to John Henry Hospital.

KENNEDY: That is rather unpleasant, isn't it, a spinal tap!

POLLARD: It was pretty bad with me.

KENNEDY: I have had a spinal tap myself. They stick that big, long needle into your spine.

Participants Endured Painful Tests

POLLARD: That is right, at John Andrew Hospital. After that, we went over early that morning, a couple of loads of us, and they taken us upstairs after giving us the spinal shot. They sit me down in the chair and the nurse and the doctor got behind and give me the shot. Then they take us upstairs in the elevators, our heels up and head down. They kept us there until five o'clock that evening, and then the nurse brought us back home.

After then, I stayed in the bed. I had taken down a day or two after I got through with the spinal tap. I stayed in bed 10 days or two weeks and the nurse came out there and give me some pills. I don't think she give me any of the medicine at that time, but just gave me some of the pills. Anyhow, she made several trips out there and I finally got in pretty good shape afterwards. It looked like my head was going back.

So after then they went to seen us once a year. They sent out notices for us to meet at Shiloh School. Sometimes they would just take the blood sample and give us some medicine right there at the school, under the oak tree where we met at Shiloh.

KENNEDY: This is a small community?

POLLARD: It is a small community.

KENNEDY: How many people are in the community?

POLLARD: Well, Tuskegee is about 12,000, but this

other little place up there I imagine is a couple thousand people there. I am about three and a half miles out.

KENNEDY: What would you do, come into town?

POLLARD: That is right, go into town.

KENNEDY: Did they have a little clinic there or a little hospital?

POLLARD: They didn't have any of that.

KENNEDY: What did you do, just meet under the tree?

POLLARD: Yes, at Shiloh School. It was about two and a half miles out. It is 10 miles between there and Tuskegee.

KENNEDY: What did they do, ask you to come back once in a while or every couple of weeks?

POLLARD: That is it. They would give us the date to come back and take those shots.

Participants Believed Treatments Were a Cure

KENNEDY: What were the shots for, to cure the bad blood?

POLLARD: Bad blood, as far as I know of.

KENNEDY: Did you think they were curing bad blood?

POLLARD: I didn't know. I just attended the clinic.

KENNEDY: They told you to keep coming back and you did?

POLLARD: When they got through giving the shots, yes. Then they give us that spinal puncture.

KENNEDY: Did they tell you why they were giving a spinal puncture?

POLLARD: No.

KENNEDY: Did you think it was because they were trying to help you?

POLLARD: To help me, yes.

KENNEDY: You wanted some help?

POLLARD: That is right. They said I had bad blood and they was working on it.

KENNEDY: How long did they keep working on it?

POLLARD: After that shot, that spinal shot—

KENNEDY: When was that?

POLLARD: That was in 1933.

KENNEDY: 1933?

POLLARD: That is right. I don't remember what month it was in, but I know it was in 1933.

KENNEDY: Did they treat you after that? Did they treat you after 1933?

POLLARD: Yes. They treat me every year. They would come down and see us every year. Of course, during that time, after I taken that spinal puncture, I wore a rubber belt around my stomach. It had a long strand around it and I would run it around, come back in front and tie it in a bow knot. They used a little ointment or salve that I rubbed on my stomach. I reckon I wore it a year or six months, something like that. After then they would see us once a year up to 25 years.

After that 25 years [of the study] they [the researchers] gave me $25.

KENNEDY: During this time, did they indicate to you what kind of treatment they were giving you, or that you were involved in any kind of test or experiment?

POLLARD: No, they never did say what it was.

KENNEDY: What did you think they were doing, just trying to cure the bad blood?

POLLARD: That is all I knew of.

KENNEDY: Did they ever take any more blood and examine it and tell you the blood was getting better?

POLLARD: They would take out blood, though.

KENNEDY: What did they tell you after they would take the blood?

POLLARD: They would just give us the pills and sometimes they would give us a little tablet to put under our tongue for sore throats. Then they would give us the green medicine for a tonic to take after meals.

KENNEDY: You thought they were treating the bad blood?

POLLARD: That is right.

KENNEDY: During this time did they ever give you any compensation or any money?

Compensation to Participants Was Inadequate

POLLARD: After that 25 years they gave me $25, a $20 and a $5 bill.

KENNEDY: After 25 years?

POLLARD: That is it. They give me a certificate.

KENNEDY: They gave you a what?

POLLARD: They gave me a certificate and a picture with six of us on there.

KENNEDY: What did the certificate say, do you remember?

POLLARD: This is one of them here in my hand.

KENNEDY: It is a certificate of merit, is it?

"U.S. Public Health Service. This certificate is awarded in grateful recognition of 25 years of participation in the Tuskegee Medical Research Study."

POLLARD: I have one of these and then I have one with a picture of five more on it.

KENNEDY: Were you glad to get it? Were you glad to get that certificate?

POLLARD: Yes.

KENNEDY: You were glad to get the $25.

POLLARD: That is right. I used the $25.

KENNEDY: Did they ever offer you anything else? Did they ever offer you any kind of free meals or free rides, anything like that?

POLLARD: No. We would have a lunch when we would go over to the Veterans Hospital. We would go to the canteen and have lunch. A lot of times I went in my own car and I would help the nurse carry the boys down there sometimes, a lot of times. I would always go in my car a lot of times.

Participants Among the Last to Know

KENNEDY: Sometime last fall [1972] did you hear or read about the experiment that was taking place, the study that was taking place on you and some of the others that were supposed to have bad blood?

POLLARD: Back last year?

KENNEDY: Yes.

POLLARD: Yes.

KENNEDY: Would you tell us a little bit about that, how you first heard about it, and what your reaction was to it?

POLLARD: The people that contacted me at the stockyard—

KENNEDY: Is that where you worked?

POLLARD: That is where I worked when they contacted me. A heavy built lady contacted me.

KENNEDY: How long have you worked at the stockyard?

POLLARD: I wasn't working out there. I was taking some cows down there last summer, my grandboy and myself.

KENNEDY: How old is he?

POLLARD: The grandboy?

KENNEDY: Yes.

POLLARD: He is 17.

KENNEDY: So you were taking some cows down to the stockyard?

POLLARD: That is it. I was taking the cows down there. A lady came up to me and asked about Charles Pollard. I looked at my grandboy and said, "I didn't know Charles Pollard. I knew Charles Wesley Pollard," and she said, "Yes, you are the one." She said she had been all over and asked about me but nobody had seen me. But I had been on the payroll bringing cows down there.

Afterwards, she told me to go ahead and get my cows unloaded and to come back out there, that she wanted to talk with me. So that is what I did.

I think they should have told. If they had told, I would have resorted to a family doctor or some other doctor.

KENNEDY: So you went out and talked to her?

POLLARD: That is right.

KENNEDY: What did she tell you?

POLLARD: She asked me wasn't I in a study or a clinic back 40 years ago. I looked at my grandboy then and he looked back. I had done forgot about it. I said, "Yes, I was in a clinic back in that time but I have done forgot about it." So she wanted to know the story of it.

You see, after them 25 years, the doctors started them two years and after that went for about three years. I haven't seen them in the last three or four years.

KENNEDY: You haven't seen them in the last three or four years?

POLLARD: No. I told her the best I could about it, what I could remember.

KENNEDY: Were you surprised when you heard about it?

POLLARD: That is right. I was surprised.

KENNEDY: Were you a little mad that you were sort of being used in a test that you didn't know about?

POLLARD: Well, at that time, you see, I didn't know nothing about it until well after I got back home. I had taken the *Birmingham News*. I have been taking it for 25 or 30 years. It was there. What I told her was in the *Birmingham News* that evening. So we read it, got to reading it, and talking about black men in Macon County. Of course, the week before then they had told in the news there about 400 or 600 men, whatever it was, the black men in Macon County, but I didn't give it even a thought, until after she told me that. That was on a Tuesday when she saw me.

Participants Were Willing to Pay for Care

KENNEDY: Have you seen any doctors since then? Have any doctors come down to see you and help you at all recently?

POLLARD: Not lately.

KENNEDY: In the last few months?

POLLARD: No. The Government doctors, no. I had been visiting a doctor, some individual doctors. Of course, I had a bad case of arthritis last year, in the last week in January. I went to Montgomery to a doctor for a month. He give an X-ray on me and sent me back to the bone specialist in Tuskegee. He doctored on me for about a month and I got on crutches and stayed on them. He finally told me to go back home. If it never did get no worse, don't come back. So I am still taking medicine, capsules that he give me. That was after he give me that shot in the hip.

KENNEDY: Did you get any bill from the doctor for seeing him about your arthritis?

POLLARD: Did I get a bill from him?

KENNEDY: Yes.

POLLARD: No, because I paid him each time.

KENNEDY: You paid him?

POLLARD: Yes, each time. That was my doctor.

KENNEDY: How much do you pay for a visit down there?

POLLARD: The X-ray cost me $25 and the medicine one time cost me $15.

KENNEDY: That one X-ray was equivalent to the $25 you got from the Government.

POLLARD: That is right. And after then I went back and got some medicine. I think I had to pay him $10 that trip. He didn't make the X-ray until to wind it up. Then he sent me back to Dr. Hume, in Tuskegee.

KENNEDY: Did you pay him, too?

POLLARD: Dr. Hume? That is right.

KENNEDY: Do you remember how much that was?

POLLARD: I paid him $15, I think, the first time. On the next trip I think I paid him $10. But I have been buying the medicine. I bought the medicine and I paid for the medicine at the desk.

KENNEDY: It runs into a lot of money, doesn't it?

POLLARD: Yes, when you go to these hospitals. Of course, back in 1961 I had an operation. I had a gland operation.

KENNEDY: Mr. Scott, would you tell us a little bit about how you heard about this?

MR. SCOTT: Yes. In 1932, we were all on the farm and going to school and Miss [Eunice] Rivers [Laurie] came out and Dr. Smith. He said he wanted to see all of us people around there, to meet at the school. So we went out and he said the purpose was to take the test of blood. So he drew blood and we went back home.

He said to be out here next Wednesday. We went back and he said, "You have bad blood and we will have to give you shots." So we would go up every week or sometimes every other week, and take shots. That is how I got involved in that. I had taken the shots for a good long while and then left the county to go to another community, but we would meet with him.

KENNEDY: How long did you take the shots?

SCOTT: We were taking those shots for about a year, almost a year.

KENNEDY: Did you receive any compensation for this?

SCOTT: I was away up in Ohio. At the time they wrote a letter to my sister and they sent $25. They said it was for the study, with Miss Rivers.

Experiment Mistaken for Treatment

KENNEDY: Is that the first time that you knew you were involved in a study?

SCOTT: I was involved in it before I left. This time, this study now, I got involved through Miss Rivers, I believe it was.

KENNEDY: What did you think they were giving the shots for?

SCOTT: Bad blood.

KENNEDY: They just told you it was for bad blood?

SCOTT: Yes.

KENNEDY: Did you think the shots were making you better?

SCOTT: I thought they would at that time.

KENNEDY: Is that what the doctor told you who gave you the shots?

SCOTT: Yes. He told me it was for bad blood.

KENNEDY: And sometime later you got the $25?

SCOTT: Yes. It was six or seven years after I left.

It is absolutely an outrageous and intolerable situation which this Government never should have been involved in.

KENNEDY: Did you get a certificate of appreciation, too?

SCOTT: No, I did not.

KENNEDY: But you heard that some of the others got it.

How did you feel after you read in the newspapers that you had been involved in this kind of study or experiment? Did that bother you at all?

SCOTT: Well, not too much at that time because I was thinking of my health, figuring they were doing me good. So I didn't think too much of it. I thought it would be all right.

And then when this study came along. I don't think much of it because I think they were just using me for something else, as an experiment.

KENNEDY: Do you think that is right?

SCOTT: No, I don't think that is right.

KENNEDY: Do you think they should have told you about it?

SCOTT: I think they should have told. If they had told, I would have resorted to a family doctor or some other doctor.

KENNEDY: You would have gone to your family doctor and got treated?

SCOTT: Yes.

KENNEDY: You thought you were being treated?

SCOTT: I thought I was being treated then.

KENNEDY: And you were not?

SCOTT: I was not.

KENNEDY: That is not right, is it?

SCOTT: No, it is not right.

Government Should Admit Responsibility

KENNEDY: What do you think the Government ought to do now?

SCOTT: I think the Government ought to do something as they were using us. They ought to give us compensation or something like that, where we can see other doctors and continue our health. That is what I think.

KENNEDY: You want to make sure that the next time you see a Government doctor that he is treating you to get you better.

SCOTT: That is right.

KENNEDY: That is what you want.

SCOTT: And I can be sure I go to the right doctor.

KENNEDY: What about you, Mr. Pollard? What would you like?

POLLARD: This I read in the paper I don't want no parts of it.

I was fixing to say I was booked to go to Birmingham when this penicillin come out, but the nurse told me I wasn't able to go up there. So they turned me down. I don't want no more part of it.

KENNEDY: Mr. Scott and Mr. Pollard, when you were talking to these doctors that were giving you these shots, did they ever suggest to you or recommend to you that you not have a family?

SCOTT: No, they did not.

POLLARD: Not what?

KENNEDY: Not have a family. Did they ever recommend to you that you not have a family?

POLLARD: No, they never said anything about that.

KENNEDY: They never mentioned that?

POLLARD: No.

Congress Admitted Government's Fault

KENNEDY: Mr. Gray, have you any further comments?

[Civil rights attorney Fred] *GRAY*: I would simply like to say, Senator Kennedy, on behalf of these participants we certainly want to express our genuine appreciation for being able to come. At least now this committee knows the views of the participants, and we certainly hope that this subcommittee and the Congress will take appropriate action to see that these people are adequately compensated.

KENNEDY: I want to thank you very much for coming. As you know several months ago, some four months ago, the Department of HEW [Health, Education and Welfare] indicated that they were going to move on this to try and remedy or rectify the situation.

The commission met on March 1 [1973] and indicated that still there had been no care forthcoming. . . . I want to indicate to you that we are going to make sure, as far as the power of this Senate Subcommittee [of the Committee on Labor and Public Welfare, 93rd Congress], that there will be help and assistance and care for all of those individuals.

It is absolutely an outrageous and intolerable situation which this Government never should have been involved in. That is bad enough, but we are going to do everything in our power to work with Mr. Pollard and Mr. Scott, and all of the others who still need the help, and the heirs of the others as well.[1]

I want to give those assurances to you, Mr. Pollard and Mr. Scott. We will look forward to working with you.

GRAY: We have waited really, Senator, about nine months on the Government to take some action before we would take any legal action. The Government simply moves very slowly and time is beginning to run out on us.

Thank you.

KENNEDY: We are going to stay after it and we will work with you. I want to thank both of you gentlemen for your appearance here, for your willingness to share with us your experience. It has been very, very helpful.

---

1. In 1974 the six hundred Tuskegee study victims and their families received a collective settlement of $10 million. In 1996 they received an apology from President Bill Clinton on behalf of the U.S. government.

5

A Tuskegee Nurse Defends Herself and the Study

Eunice Rivers Laurie, interviewed by A. Lillian Thompson

Eunice Rivers Laurie was an African American nurse who recruited men to participate in the Tuskegee study. The following selection is an interview Laurie gave to A. Lillian Thompson, a researcher with the *Black Women Oral History Project*. Although Laurie received heavy criticism for recruiting African American men into a study that would result in their disease going untreated, she vigorously defends the study. In answer to the accusation that many of the men were never actually treated for syphilis, she tells Thompson that the disease was already too advanced in many participants for them to have benefited from treatment. She also defends the study by pointing out that many of the men would not have been able to afford the high quality of medical care they received as a result of their participation. Laurie notes that she had intervened to make sure that the white doctors spoke respectfully to their African American patients. The *Black Women Oral History Project* was produced under the direction of the Schlesinger Library of Radcliffe College.

A. Lillian Thompson: When you stopped working for the Movable School,[1] then what did you do? How did you happen to leave?

1. Before working for the Tuskegee study, Laurie worked with the Movable School project, which was a bus equipped for teaching people in various locations how to sew, cook, and clean.

Eunice Rivers Laurie, interviewed by A. Lillian Thompson, *The Black Women Oral History Project*. Westport, CT: Meckler, 1991. Copyright © 2005 by the Associated Press. All rights reserved. Distributed by Valeo IP.

Eunice Rivers Laurie: Really and truly. I got with this syphilitic program that was sort of a hoodwink thing, I suppose. Not hoodwink, I don't mean it like that. But at that particular time, Macon County [Alabama] was overrun with syphilis and gonorrhea. In fact, the rate of syphilis in the Negro was very, very high, something like eighty percent or something like this. The argument, as I remember, was that the white man had neurosyphilis—that was infections of the spinal cord, these nerves and all. The Negro died with whatever the other one is—maybe I can remember. But anyway, the Negro had syphilis which affected his heart and liver, and organs of the body more so than the white man. The white man had neurosyphilis that was syphilis of the nerves. And at that time Macon County was overrun with syphilis. They had the highest rate of anybody in any of the southern counties.

A lot of things that have been written have been unfair.

How was this known? Were they routinely giving them blood tests, as to how it was diagnosed?

Well, I was going to say now how I got into this and how they found them. They were making this study, and they were comparing this study with a study of syphilis that was made in Norway, I believe. And they found that the white man there had neurosyphilis. Then they wanted to make a comparison. At that particular time, as I said, syphilis was rampant in Macon County. I think Macon County had the highest rate, and of course, at that particular time among Negroes, that could be. So then they wanted to do this study, so . . . how did I get into it now? I'm just trying to think, but anyway, maybe I'll back up and get to it. They wanted a nurse to work with them. . . . I was just interested. I mean I wanted to get into everything that I possibly could. So he said, "Well, do you want to take it? I think you'd be good." And I said, "Yeah, whatever I can do with it."

So then they came down from Washington, these doctors came from Washington. We went from community to community in Macon County, drawing blood, and treating the positive patients. Well, all patients were getting treatment, all of them, except these people who were included in the study. We had this bus that was equipped to go from community to community. It was a regular clinic, everything was sterilized. Preparation of your medicine, everything was on this bus. The people would meet us, say, here at my house. Ten or fifteen people would be here. This would be one center. And we'd stop in and give treatment and draw blood. And so out of that grew this study, this VD [venereal disease] study.

And so then after we got started with the study, they employed me, they wanted me to work with them. The people from Washington wanted me to work with them. That was just up my alley; it didn't get monotonous either. So then Dr. Smith asked me, "Nurse Rivers, would you like to work with Dr. Wenger and them on the bus?" . . . Dr. Wenger was one of these fussy folks, just fussy, just plain fussy; Dr. Smith said, "you are about the only one who can get along with him." I said, "Well, he don't make me no difference. I know what I'm doing, and I hope he knows what he is doing; it don't make any difference to me. He can yell all he wants. I don't even hear him." He said, "That's good, that's good, Nurse Rivers, that's good." I said, "I don't even hear him, Dr. Smith." I said, "Are you ready? I know I'm doing my work. He can rant all he wants to, he'll be the one dying of high blood pressure, not me." He laughed at that. . . . So that's how I transferred to them. The state didn't want me to leave them, but I insisted. I was tired of that. I wanted to get into this. So this is how I got into this venereal disease study and worked with them. That started in 1932. So what the study consisted of, we had a positive group and a negative group. We had 400 positive groups and 200 negative groups that we studied. . . .

This is the thing that really hurt me about the unfair publicity. Those people had been given better medical care than some of us who could afford it.

Was this confined to Macon County or throughout the state?
No, not throughout the state, some of the adjoining counties, we had people who would come over to us. From another county they would come in, but we didn't go out-

side of Macon County to hunt patients. If they lived on the border, and they came over, then they became eligible for the study, then they could come on in. We had several people who lived up around Auburn, some from Montgomery. But they came to us, we didn't go to them. They started out . . . having these people to meet us at these places where we would treat them. And after we drew their blood, and the doctors got a history on them, then they would decide who was who, whether he went to this side. But the patients were always asked if they wanted to come on this side or go on to the other side, see. And they never took anybody with early syphilis. And early syphilis was about three years or two years, that's considered early. After that, it was supposed to be late syphilis. What it was doing, it was doing it to you, you weren't transmitting it, see.

Participants Got Superior Medical Treatment

So this is how we got the study. We tried to match the age group on both sides, so many under fifty, this kind of thing. And with the study, the doctors would come down once about every two years and spend about three or four months in the county visiting, examining, X-raying. Honestly, those people got all kinds of examinations and medical care that they never would have gotten. I've taken them over to the hospital and they'd have a GI [gastro-intestinal] series on them, the heart, the lung, just everything. It was just impossible for just an ordinary person to get that kind of an examination.

Quite a bit has been written about that study over the last several years. How do you feel about the types of things that have been written?

A lot of things that have been written have been unfair. A lot of things. We did not take cases that were early cases. Syphilis had done its damage with most of the people, see. And this was another thing that we had found. Now, they say that with the white man, syphilis effects the mind and this and that, but the doctors themselves have said that the study has proven that syphilis did not affect the Negro as it did the white man, you see. So this is the way it affected the people. And according to this study, there was always a question in their minds, I really don't think they ever have definitely decided, what and how, if it was as bad as has actually been said, you see.

How did this project end? That is, your participation with this assignment?

Well, it ended a couple of years ago when they started all of this publicity.

It lasted right up until that time? Were they still actively bringing people into the project?

Doctors came down, not every year, but about every two years. To begin with, they came down once a year after they had gone back. They would send a group of doctors down here and they would stay about two weeks or so, as long as they were needed. And they would examine and see the patients. They had a little medication for them. A lot of them at that particular time had poor appetites and poor blood, not enough iron in it. They furnished us with iron and that kind of thing, and tonics. So that the doctors came about every two years.

Participants Never Lost Faith in Rivers

Then as the study grew and the patients grew older, they would come every year. Come down and spend two or three weeks with them. And honestly, those patients got good medical care. This is the thing that always hurt me, how they criticized. Those people would come down here and they'd get all kinds of extra things, cardiograms and . . . some of the things that I had never heard of. This is the thing that really hurt me about the unfair publicity. Those people had been given better medical care than some of us who could afford it.

What about their families' reaction, as it relates to you? Have they believed the press or have they still maintained their trust in you?

No. They love Mrs. Rivers.

So they understand?

In all of this that has gone on, I have never heard anyone say anything that was bad about it. The funny thing about it is, sometimes they'd send these young doctors down and they would be short, you know how these young folk are. They were talking to the patients and saying, "You do so and so." "What, you crazy?" And I would go in there and get them. I said, "Now, we don't talk to our patients like this." I said, "They're human. You don't talk to them like that." I said, "I'm sorry." They'd calm down. This particular patient said, "Mrs. Rivers, go in there and tell that white man to stop talking to us like that." I had two white doctors who apologized. They said, "Miss Laurie, I didn't mean it like it sounded. I guess I was kind of upset." I said, "Well, you sounded terrible. I hope you don't do that any more, 'cause they are all human." I said, "If anything happens that you can't get along, that you can't get it through their head, just call me. We'll straighten it out. But don't holler at them." I said, "These are grown men; some of them are old men. Don't holler at them."

6

The United States Apologizes for the Tuskegee Study

William J. Clinton

In May 1997, sixty-five years after the Tuskegee syphilis study began, President William J. (Bill) Clinton publicly apologized to a gathering of surviving study participants and their families on behalf of the U.S. government. In the following speech, not only does he acknowledge that the government-funded researchers betrayed the men who believed they were receiving treatment for their disease, but he also promises the participants that no others will ever be similarly abused in the name of medical science. In addition, Clinton announces that the government will fund several projects to ensure ethical medical research practices, including the development of a center for bioethics at the Tuskegee Institute.

L adies and gentlemen, on Sunday, Mr. [Herman] Shaw will celebrate his 95th birthday. I would like to recognize the other survivors who are here today and their families: Mr. Charlie Pollard is here. Mr. Carter Howard. Mr. Fred Simmons. Mr. Simmons just took his first airplane ride, and he reckons he's about 110 years old, so I think it's time for him to take a chance or two. I'm glad he did. And Mr. Frederick Moss, thank you, sir.

I would also like to ask three family representatives who are here—Sam Doner is represented by his daughter, Gwen-

William J. Clinton, address in the East Room, Washington, DC, May 16, 1997.

dolyn Cox. Thank you, Gwendolyn. Ernest Hendon, who is watching in Tuskegee, is represented by his brother, North Hendon. Thank you, sir, for being here. And George Key is represented by his grandson, Christopher Monroe. Thank you, Chris. . . .

America Must Not Forget Tuskegee

The eight men who are survivors of the syphilis study at Tuskegee are a living link to a time not so very long ago that many Americans would prefer not to remember, but we dare not forget. It was a time when our nation failed to live up to its ideals, when our nation broke the trust with our people that is the very foundation of our democracy. It is not only in remembering that shameful past that we can make amends and repair our nation, but it is in remembering that past that we can build a better present and a better future. And without remembering it, we cannot make amends and we cannot go forward.

So today America does remember the hundreds of men used in research without their knowledge and consent. We remember them and their family members. Men who were poor and African American, without resources and with few alternatives, they believed they had found hope when they were offered free medical care by the United States Public Health Service. They were betrayed.

And without remembering [the shame of the Tuskegee study], we cannot make amends and we cannot go forward.

Medical people are supposed to help when we need care, but even once a cure was discovered, they were denied help, and they were lied to by their government. Our government is supposed to protect the rights of its citizens; their rights were trampled upon. Forty years, hundreds of men betrayed, along with their wives and children, along with the community in Macon County, Alabama, the City of Tuskegee, the fine university there, and the larger African American community.

The United States government did something that was wrong—deeply, profoundly, morally wrong. It was an outrage to our commitment to integrity and equality for all our citizens.

To the survivors, to the wives and family members, the children and the grandchildren, I say what you know: No power on Earth can give you back the lives lost, the pain suffered, the years of internal torment and anguish. What was done cannot be undone. But we can end the silence. We can stop turning our heads away. We can look at you in the eye and finally say on behalf of the American people, what the United States government did was shameful, and I am sorry.

The American people are sorry—for the loss, for the years of hurt. You did nothing wrong, but you were grievously wronged. I apologize and I am sorry that this apology has been so long in coming.

The United States government did something that was wrong—deeply, profoundly, morally wrong.

To Macon County, to Tuskegee, to the doctors who have been wrongly associated with the events there, you have our apology, as well. To our African American citizens, I am sorry that your federal government orchestrated a study so clearly racist. That can never be allowed to happen again. It is against everything our country stands for and what we must stand against is what it was.

So let us resolve to hold forever in our hearts and minds the memory of a time not long ago in Macon County, Alabama, so that we can always see how adrift we can become when the rights of any citizens are neglected, ignored and betrayed. And let us resolve here and now to move forward together.

We Must Pay Greater Attention to Medical Ethics

The legacy of the study at Tuskegee has reached far and deep, in ways that hurt our progress and divide our nation. We cannot be one America when a whole segment of our nation has no trust in America. An apology is the first step, and we take it with a commitment to rebuild that broken trust. We can begin by making sure there is never again another episode like this one. We need to do more to ensure that medical research practices are sound and ethical, and that researchers work more closely with communities.

Today I would like to announce several steps to help us achieve these goals. First, we will help to build that lasting memorial at Tuskegee. The school founded by Booker T. Washington [writer and civil rights advocate, 1858–1915], distinguished by the renowned scientist George Washington Carver [1864–1943] and so many others who advanced the health and well-being of African Americans and all Americans, is a fitting site. The Department of Health and Human Services will award a planning grant so the school can pursue establishing a center for bioethics in research and health care. The center will serve as a museum of the study and support efforts to address its legacy and strengthen bioethics training.

The people who ran the study at Tuskegee diminished the stature of man by abandoning the most basic ethical precepts.

Second, we commit to increase our community involvement so that we may begin restoring lost trust. The study at Tuskegee served to sow distrust of our medical institutions, especially where research is involved. Since the study was halted, abuses have been checked by making informed consent and local review mandatory in federally funded and mandated research.

African Americans to Play Larger Role

Still, 25 years later, many medical studies have little African American participation and African American organ donors are few. This impedes efforts to conduct promising research and to provide the best health care to all our people, including African Americans. So today, I'm directing the Secretary of Health and Human Services, Donna Shalala, to issue a report in 180 days about how we can best involve communities, especially minority communities, in research and health care. You must—every American group must be involved in medical research in ways that are positive. We have put the curse behind us; now we must bring the bene-fits to all Americans.

Third, we commit to strengthen researchers' training in bioethics. We are constantly working on making break-throughs in protecting the health of our people and in van-quishing diseases. But all our people must be assured that their rights and dignity will be respected as new drugs, treat-ments and therapies are tested and used. So I am directing Secretary Shalala to work in partnership with higher educa-tion to prepare training materials for medical researchers. They will be available in a year. They will help researchers build on core ethical principles of respect for individuals, jus-tice and informed consent, and advise them on how to use these principles effectively in diverse populations.

Fourth, to increase and broaden our understanding of ethical issues and clinical research, we commit to providing postgraduate fellowships to train bioethicists especially among African Americans and other minority groups. HHS [Health and Human Services] will offer these fellowships beginning in September of 1998 to promising students en-rolled in bioethics graduate programs.

And, finally, by executive order I am also today extend-ing the charter of the National Bioethics Advisory Com-mission to October of 1999. The need for this commission is clear. We must be able to call on the thoughtful, collec-tive wisdom of experts and community representatives to find ways to further strengthen our protections for subjects in human research.

A Challenge to the Medical Community

We face a challenge in our time. Science and technology are rapidly changing our lives with the promise of making us much healthier, much more productive and more prosper-ous. But with these changes we must work harder to see that as we advance we don't leave behind our conscience. No ground is gained and, indeed, much is lost if we lose our moral bearings in the name of progress.

The people who ran the study at Tuskegee diminished the stature of man by abandoning the most basic ethical precepts. They forgot their pledge to heal and repair. They had the power to heal the survivors and all the others and they did not. Today, all we can do is apologize. But you have the power, for only you—Mr. Shaw, the others who are

here, the family members who are with us in Tuskegee—
only you have the power to forgive. Your presence here
shows us that you have chosen a better path than your government did so long ago. You have not withheld the power
to forgive. I hope today and tomorrow every American will
remember your lesson and live by it.

Chapter 2

The Willowbrook Hepatitis Study

1

Infectious Hepatitis

Saul Krugman, Joan P. Giles, and Jack Hammond

In 1967 lead Willowbrook researcher Saul Krugman and his colleagues Joan P. Giles and Jack Hammond submitted the following article describing the study's purpose and their ethical considerations in designing it. First, they offer a defense of human hepatitis experiments as the only way of discovering a cure. Second, they emphasize that since hepatitis was uncontrolled at Willowbrook, the children they artificially injected with the virus would have inevitably contracted a much more virulent form of it. They also point out that the children were then isolated in a "special" ward with medical and nursing personnel to give them careful attention. Finally, they include a section of the World Medical Association's Draft Code of Ethics on Experimentation, which they say they followed to the letter.

Infectious hepatitis has been recognized as an endemic disease at the Willowbrook State School, Staten Island, NY, since 1953. As a result of this endemic environment, 1,153 cases of infectious hepatitis with jaundice were observed to have been transmitted by natural contact in this institution during the past 12 years. Second attacks with jaundice have occurred in 63 patients or 5.5% of this group. In most instances the second attack of jaundice occurred within one year but occasionally as late as four and seven years after the first attack. One possible explanation for second attacks would be the existence of multiple types of infectious hepatitis virus, immunologically separate and distinct. Examples

Saul Krugman, Joan P. Giles, and Jack Hammond, "Infectious Hepatitis: Evidence for Two Distinctive Clinical, Epidemiological, and Immunological Types of Infection," *The Journal of the American Medical Association*, vol. 200, May 1, 1967. Reproduced by permission.

of this phenomenon have been observed in inferovirus, adenovirus, and myxovirus infections. The studies reported in this communication provide evidence for the presence of two distinctive clinical, epidemiological, and immunological types of infectious hepatitis.

The benefits of such a program to the entire institution were obvious.

The nature of the endemic situation at the Willowbrook State School has been described in detail in previous reports. Briefly, infectious hepatitis was first noticed among Willowbrook patients as early as 1949. From 1949 to 1963 the patient population increased from a mere 200 to over 6,000. As the population increased and new susceptible children were admitted, hepatitis found a continuous foothold. Attempts to relieve overcrowding have now reduced this population to approximately 5,400 mentally retarded patients, predominantly children, who are distributed among 24 buildings. The constant admission of many susceptible children and the natural transmission of the disease via the intestinal-oral route have been responsible for the continuing endemic situation. Many of the patients are incapable of being toilet trained and prone to put everything that they pick up into their mouths. This intensifies the problem of control. Under the chronic circumstance of multiple and repeated natural exposure, it has been shown that most newly admitted children become infected within the first 6 to 12 months of residence in the institution.

The Study Was Necessary

Prior experience indicated that γ-globulin [gamma globulin] did not prevent hepatitis infection; it attenuated [shortened] the disease. Eleven separate dosage trials with γ-globulin have been undertaken since 1956 in an attempt to reduce the number of clinical cases of infectious hepatitis in the institution. The direct measurable result of these programs was a reduction of approximately 85% of icteric [related to jaundice] hepatitis among patients and employees at Willowbrook. With the realization that subclinical cases persisted and were contagious, elimination of the disease could not be accomplished. In the absence of an effective vaccine, the study on the natural history of infectious hepatitis in this institution was therefore considered an important step toward better understanding and future control of this infection. The benefits of such a program to the entire institution were obvious. It remained then to assess the risks and the benefits to the children who would be active participants in the study.

The Study Was Designed to Minimize Danger

The decision to propose the controlled infection of a small number of newly admitted children was based on the following considerations:

1. It was well recognized that infectious hepatitis was a mild and relatively benign disease in children as compared with adults. . . . Experience at Willowbrook indicated that the disease observed at this institution was especially mild. Consequently, only the Willowbrook strains of infectious hepatitis virus would be used for the study.

2. The study group would include only children whose parents gave written consent after being informed of the details, potential risks, and potential benefits of the investigation.

3. The study would be carried out in a special isolation unit with special medical and nursing personnel to provide close observation and optimum care. Thus, these children would be protected from other endemic diseases in the institution, such as shigellosis [intestinal disorder caused by a parasite], parasitic infections, respiratory infections, and other infectious diseases. Experience has indicated that the children in the special isolation unit were subjected to *less* risk than the children who were admitted directly to the institutional wards.

4. It is important to emphasize that the studies were to be carried out at the Willowbrook State School because of the local endemic situation, and *not* because the children were mentally retarded.

Observations on approximately 250 children who acquired artificially induced hepatitis in the Willowbrook study since 1956 revealed that the experimental disease was generally milder than the observed natural infection. In fact, many cases would have gone unrecognized if it had not been for careful daily observation and serial biochemical tests of liver function.

The studies were reviewed and sanctioned by the University Committee on Human Experimentation, by the New York State Department of Mental Hygiene, and by the Armed Forces Epidemiological Board. The Willowbrook studies have been conducted in accordance with the World Medical Association's Draft Code of Ethics on Human Experimentation. The guidelines which were adopted for the study at its inception in 1956 conform with the following general principles of the Code of Ethics: (1) that where children are to be the subject of an experiment, the nature, the reason, and risks of it should be fully explained to their parents or lawful guardians, who should have complete freedom to make a decision on behalf of the children; (2) that children in institutions and not under the care of relatives should not be the subject of human experiment; (3) that the experiment should be conducted only by scientifically qualified persons and under the supervision of a qualified medical man; (4) that during the course of the experiment the subject of it should be free to withdraw from it at any time; (5) that the investigator, or investigating committee, or any scientifically or medically qualified person associated with him or the committee should be free to discontinue the experiment if in his or their judgment it may, if continued, be harmful to the subject of the experiment; (6) that any risk to which the subject of an experiment may be exposed should be carefully assessed in terms of direct benefit to himself or indirect benefit to others, on the assumption that the risks have been explained to, and freely accepted by, the subject of the experiment.

2

The Willowbrook Study Was Extremely Unethical

Paul Ramsey

In his book *The Patient as Person: Explorations in Medical Ethics*, theologian and medical ethicist Paul Ramsey does concede that Saul Krugman and his colleagues undertook the Willowbrook study only after "much soul-searching." However, he sharply criticizes their research. He argues that it was unethical to experiment on a captive population of mentally ill and thus extremely vulnerable children. Ramsey also maintains that the researchers misrepresented the study from the beginning. All involved were led to believe that the study would be conducted as a method of controlling hepatitis in the institution. In actuality, the researchers did not take measures to prevent the spread of the disease. Their only intention was to investigate hepatitis and discover a vaccine for it. In addition, Ramsey points out that the researchers deceived parents who who were under extreme pressure to find adequate care for their severely disabled children. These parents were told that Willowbrook only had openings for new children in its "hepatitis research unit" and were given incomplete and inaccurate information about the experiments and the long-term effects they could have on their children. Paul Ramsey is the author of *Basic Christian Ethics, Christian Ethics and the Sit-In, Life or Death: Ethics and Options, Ethics of Fetal Research*, and *Ethics at the Edges of Life*.

In 1958 and 1959 the *New England Journal of Medicine* reported a series of experiments performed upon patients and new admittees to the Willowbrook State School, a home for retarded children in Staten Island, New York. These experiments were described as "an attempt to control the high prevalence of infectious hepatitis in an institution for mentally defective patients." The experiments were said to be justified because, under conditions of an existing controlled outbreak of hepatitis in the institution, "knowledge obtained from a series of suitable studies could well lead to its control." In actuality, the experiments were designed to duplicate and confirm the efficacy of gamma globulin [blood protein rich in disease antibodies] in immunization against hepatitis, to develop and improve or improve upon that inoculum [material used for inoculation], and to learn more about infectious hepatitis in general.

Nothing requires that major research into the natural history of hepatitis be first undertaken in children.

The experiments were justified—doubtless, after a great deal of soul searching—for the following reasons: there was a smoldering epidemic throughout the institution and "it was apparent that most of the patients at Willowbrook were naturally exposed to hepatitis virus"; infectious hepatitis is a much milder disease in children; the strain at Willowbrook was especially mild; only the strain or strains of the virus already disseminated at Willowbrook were used: and only those small and incompetent patients whose parents gave consent were used. . . .

The Study Was Ethically Flawed

Serious ethical questions may be raised about the trials so far described. No mention is made of any attempt to enlist the adult personnel of the institution, numbering nearly 1,000 including nearly 600 attendants on ward duty, and new additions to the staff, in these studies whose excusing reason was that almost everyone was "naturally" exposed to the Willowbrook virus. Nothing requires that major research into the natural history of hepatitis be first undertaken in children. Experiments have been carried out in the military and with prisoners as subjects. There have been fatalities from the experiments; but surely in all these cases the consent of the volunteers was as valid or better than the proxy consent of these children's "representatives." There would have been no question of the understanding consent that might have been given by the adult personnel at Willowbrook, if significant benefits were expected from studying that virus.

Second, nothing is said that would warrant withholding an inoculation of some degree of known efficacy from part of the population, or for withholding in the first trial less than the full amount of gamma globulin that had served to immunize in previous tests, except the need to test, confirm, and improve the inoculum. That, of course, was a desirable goal; but it does not seem possible to warrant withholding gamma globulin for the reason that is often said to justify controlled trials, namely, that one procedure is *as likely* to succeed as the other.

The special moral claims of children for care and protection are forgotten, and especially the claims of children who are most weak and vulnerable.

Third, nothing is said about attempts to control or defeat the low-grade epidemic at Willowbrook by more ordinary, if more costly and less experimental, procedures. Nor is anything said about admitting no more patients until this goal had been accomplished. This was not a massive urban hospital whose teeming population would have to be turned out into the streets, with resulting dangers to themselves and to public health, in order to sanitize the place. Instead, between 200 and 250 patients were housed in each of 18 buildings over approximately 400 acres in a semirural setting of fields, woods, and well-kept, spacious lawns. Clearly it would have been possible to secure other accommodation for new admissions away from the infection, while eradicating the infection at Willowbrook building by building. This might have cost money, and it would certainly have required astute detective work to discover the source of the infection. The doctors determined that the new patients likely were not carrying the infection upon admission, and that it did not arise from the procedures and routine inoculations given them at the time of admission. Why not go further in the search for the source of the epidemic? If this had been an orphanage for normal children or a floor of private patients, instead of a school for mentally defective children, one wonders whether the doctors would so readily have accepted the hepatitis as a "natural" occurrence and even as an opportunity for study.

The Effects of the Study Were Understated

The next step was to attempt to induce "passive-active immunity" by feeding the virus to patients already protected by gamma globulin. In this attempt to improve the inoculum, permission was obtained from the parents of children from 5 to 10 years of age newly admitted to Willowbrook, who were then isolated from contact with the rest of the institution. All were inoculated with gamma globulin and then divided into two groups: one served as controls [those not given the virus] while the other group of new patients were fed the Willowbrook virus, obtained from feces, in doses having 50 percent infectivity, i.e., in concentrations estimated to produce hepatitis with jaundice in half the subjects tested. Then twice the 50 percent infectivity was tried. This proved, among other things, that hepatitis has an "alimentary-tract [digestive system] phase" in which it can be transmitted from one person to another while still "inapparent" in the first person. This, doubtless, is exceedingly important information in learning how to control epidemics of infectious hepatitis. The second of the two articles mentioned above describes studies of the incubation period of the virus and of whether pooled serum remained infectious when aged and frozen. Still the small, mentally defective patients who were deliberately fed infectious hepatitis are described as having suffered mildly in most cases: "The liver became enlarged in the majority, occasionally a week or two before the onset of jaundice. Vomiting and anorexia usually lasted only a few days. Most of the children gained weight during the course of hepatitis."

That mild description of what happened to the children who were fed hepatitis (and who continued to be introduced into the unaltered environment of Willowbrook) is itself alarming, since it is now definitely known that cirrhosis [incurable disease of liver tissue] . . . results from infectious hepatitis more frequently than from excessive consumption of alcohol! Now, or in 1958 and 1959, no one knows what may be other serious consequences of contracting infectious hepatitis. Understanding human volunteers were then and are now needed in the study of this disease, although a South American monkey has now successfully been given a form of hepatitis, and can henceforth serve as our ally in its conquest. But not children who cannot consent knowingly. If Peace Corps workers are regularly given gamma globulin before going abroad as a guard against their contracting hepatitis, and are inoculated at intervals thereafter, it seems that this is the least we should do for mentally defective children before they "go abroad" to Willowbrook or other institutions set up for their care.

The Study Justifications Were Flimsy

Discussions pro and con of the Willowbrook experiments that have come to my attention serve only to reinforce the ethical objections that can be raised against what was done simply from a careful analysis of the original articles reporting the research design and findings. In an address at the 1968 Ross Conference on Pediatric Research, Dr. Saul Krugman [one of the Willowbrook researchers] raised the question, Should vaccine trials be carried out in adult volunteers before subjecting children to similar tests? He answered this question in the negative. The reason adduced was simply that "a vaccine virus trial may be a more hazardous procedure for adults than for children." Medical researchers, of course, are required to minimize the hazards, but not by moving from consenting to unconsenting subjects. This apology clearly shows that adults and children have become interchangeable in face of the overriding importance of obtaining the research goal. This means that the special moral claims of children for care and protection are forgotten, and especially the claims of children who are most weak and vulnerable. . . .

The *Medical Tribune* explains that the 16-bed isolation unit set up at Willowbrook served "to protect the study subjects from Willowbrook's other endemic [localized] diseases—such as shigellosis, measles, rubella and respiratory and parasitic infections—while exposing them to hepatitis." This presumably compensated for the infection they were given. It is not convincingly shown that the children could by no means, however costly, have been protected from the epidemic of hepatitis. The statement that Willowbrook "had endemic infectious hepatitis and a sufficiently open population so that the disease could never be quieted by exhausting the supply of susceptibles" is at best enigmatic [confusing].

Oddly, physicians defending the propriety of the Willowbrook hepatitis project soon begin talking like poorly instructed "natural lawyers"! Dr. Louis Lasagna and Dr. Geoffrey Edsall, for example, find these experiments unobjectionable—both, for the reason stated by Edsall: "the children would apparently incur no greater risk than they were likely to run by nature." In any case, Edsall's examples of parents consenting with a son 17 years of age for him to go to war, and society's agreement with minors that they can drive cars and hurt themselves were entirely beside the point. Dr. David D. Rutstein adheres to a stricter standard in regard to research on infectious hepatitis: "It is not ethical to use human subjects for the growth of a virus for any purpose."

Such use of captive populations of children for purely experimental purposes ought to be made legally impossible.

The latter sweeping verdict may depend on knowledge of the effects of viruses on chromasomal difficulties, mongolism, etc., that was not available to the Willowbrook group when their researches were begun thirteen years ago. If so, this is a telling point against appeal to "no discernible risks" as the sole standard applicable to the use of children in medical experimentation. That would lend support to the proposition that we always know that there are unknown and undiscerned risks in the case of an invasion of the fortress of the body—which then can be consented to by an adult in behalf of a child only if it is in the child's behalf medically.

When asked what she told the parents of the subject-children at Willowbrook, Dr. Joan Giles replied, "I explain that there is no vaccine against infectious hepatitis. . . . I also tell them that we can modify the disease with gamma globulin but we can't provide lasting immunity without letting them get the disease." Obviously vaccines giving "lasting immunity" are not the only kinds of vaccine to be used in caring for patients.

Benefits Did Not Outweigh Risks

Doubtless the studies at Willowbrook resulted in improvement in the vaccine, to the benefit of present and future patients. In September 1966, "a routine program of GG [gamma globulin] administration to every new patient at Willowbrook" was begun. This cut the incidence of icteric hepatitis 80 to 85 percent. Then follows a significant statement in the *Medical Tribune* article: "A similar reduction in the icteric form of the disease has been accomplished among the employees, who began getting routine GG earlier in the study." Not only did the research team (so far as these reports show) fail to consider and adopt the alternative that new admittees to the staff be asked to become volunteers for an investigation that might improve the vaccine against the strand of infectious hepatitis to which they as well as the children were exposed. Instead, the staff was routinely protected earlier than the inmates were! And, as we have seen, there was evidence from the beginning that gamma globulin provided at least some protection. A "modification" of the disease was still an inoculum, even if this provided no lasting immunization and had to be repeated. It is axiomatic to medical ethics that a known remedy or protection—even if not perfect or even if the best exact administration of it has not been proved—should not be withheld from individual patients. It seems to a layman that from the beginning various trials at immunization of all new admittees might have been made, and controlled observation made of their different degrees of effectiveness against "nature" at Willowbrook. This would doubtless have been a longer way round, namely, the "anecdotal" method of investigative treatment that comes off second best in comparison with controlled trials. Yet this seems to be the alternative dictated by our received medical ethics, and the only one expressive of minimal care of the primary patients themselves.

Parents Had Little Choice

Finally, except for one episode the obtaining of parental consent (on the premise that this is ethically valid) seems to have been very well handled. Wards of the state were not used, though by law the administrator at Willowbrook could have signed consent for them. Only new admittees whose parents were available were entered by proxy consent into the project. Explanation was made to groups of these parents, and they were given time to think about it and consult with their own family physicians. Then late in 1964 Willowbrook was closed to all new admissions because of overcrowding. What then happened can most impartially be described in the words of an article [that appeared in the *Medical Tribune* on February 20, 1967] defending the Willowbrook project on medical and ethical grounds:

> Parents who applied for their children to get in were sent a form letter over Dr. Hammond's signature saying that there was no space for new admissions and that their name was being put on a waiting list.

> But the hepatitis program, occupying its own space in the institution, continued to admit new patients as each new study group began. "Where do you find new admissions except by canvassing the people who have applied for admission?" Dr. Hammond asked.

> So a new batch of form letters went out, saying that there were a few vacancies in the hepatitis research unit if the parents cared to consider volunteering their child for that.

> In some instances the second form letter apparently was received as closely as a week after the first letter arrived.

Granting—as I do not—the validity of parental consent to research upon children not in their behalf medically, what sort of consent was that? Surely, the duress [pressure] upon these parents with children so defective as to require institutionalization was far greater than the duress on prisoners given tobacco or paid or promised parole for their cooperation. I grant that the timing of these events was inadvertent. Since, however, ethics is a matter of criticizing institutions and not only of exculpating [clearing from guilt] or making culprits of individual men, the inadvertence does not matter. This is the strongest possible argument for saying that even if parents have the right to consent to submit the children who are directly and continuously in their care to nonbeneficial medical experimentation, this should not be the rule of practice governing institutions set up for their care.

Such use of captive populations of children for purely experimental purposes ought to be made legally impossible.

My view is that this should be stopped by legal acknowledgment of the moral invalidity of parental or legal proxy consent for the child to procedures having no relation to a child's own diagnosis or treatment. If this is not done, canons of loyalty require that the rule of practice (by law, or otherwise) be that children in institutions and not directly under the care of parents or relatives should *never* be used in medical investigations having present pain or discomfort and unknown present and future risks to them, and promising future possible benefits only for others.

3

The Willowbrook Researchers Acted Ethically

Joan P. Giles

In response to heavy criticism from the medical community about the Willowbrook study, Joan P. Giles, a physician with the Department of Pediatrics at New York University Medical Center and a researcher in the Willowbrook study, offers a defense of herself and her colleagues in the following letter to the editor of the medical journal the *Lancet*. Although she welcomes an examination of the ethics of the study, she faults her critics for oversimplifying complex moral issues. She states that it is not unethical to study a disease already running rampant in an institutional setting. Giles counters the criticism that she and fellow researchers did nothing to stem the disease's spread by saying that studying it in a systematic way contributed to its control and, in turn, eased the suffering of the children bound to be infected by it. She also argues that the researchers only infected and studied children whose parents consented to the study. She maintains that she and fellow researchers, as must all individuals in their position, did what their consciences told them was morally right in conducting the study. Giles joined the Willowbrook research team in 1955 and remained with the study until 1972. She died in 1973.

No man has yet known absolute right or absolute wrong. We are grateful to those who would have us review, to examine our ethics. Let us go back.

Joan P. Giles, "Hepatitis Research Among Retarded Children," *The Lancet*, vol. 1, May 29, 1971. Copyright © 1971 by The Lancet Ltd. Reproduced with permission from Elsevier.

The institutional problem does not begin with endemicity [localized disease] and its morbid toll. It begins with heredity, prenatal and postnatal infection, prenatal and postnatal trauma. So do its ethics. The compounding of moral decisions that precede institutionalisation give us pause. The geneticist, weighing adverse chance with fact and figures, advises that a handicapped child should not be conceived: the parents, informed, accept or reject such advice. The therapeutic abortionist, equally fundamental, equally weighing adverse chance with fact and figures, advises that a handicapped fetus should not be born: the parents, informed, accept or reject such advice. The obstetrician, knowledgeable though fallible, makes decisions according to his best judgment: the parents, informed, accept or defer to his decisions. The pædiatric surgeon must do the same, weighing knowledge and success against adverse chance: the parents, informed, accept or reject his advice. The physician, religious leader, or social worker who advises removal of the retarded child from the home his presence disrupts must weigh the repercussions [possibly harsh results] of moral responsibility. The parents who accept this advice must answer to their conscience. In each case the skilled, the knowledgeable physician, informs, advises; in each case, from before conception to day of admission to an institution, it is the parents who ultimately decide: an awesome precedent. The physician does not make the moral judgment. He stands by, ultimately human, to accept or reject parental decision. If he cannot accept, he refers. If he accepts, he acts.

Willowbrook Researchers Weighed Many Factors

All this we inherit as institutionalisation begins: to understand, not to judge, to give support during the necessary period of adjustment, to feel the weight of adverse chance, to inform of the statistical realities which, our knowledge tells us, have not ended with admission. We have learned through the mass of case-histories, and through listening, the presumption of moral judgment in areas of our own reprieve.

We too are dealing with facts, with adverse chance, with, to be specific, our problem: endemicity of hepatitis. We too must await the ultimate parental decision: controlled or uncontrolled exposure, immunity safely by design through minimal disease, or by natural endemic exposure, ill-timed perhaps, with the adverse chance of complicating with respiratory disease, shigellosis, Cox-sackie or echoviruses: the compounded infections which threaten survival. We are physicians, dedicated to life, to support, to teach, to grow with our knowledge, to offer more because of this knowledge; and because of overwhelming circumstances we knew that action was warranted. We too believe that it is the duty of the pædiatrician to attempt to improve the situation. Put back the knowledge gained and we must deal, in conscience, with ignorance. This too begets reaction. We could have stepped over disease and been blamed for not caring. As a matter of record, instead we have slowly and carefully advanced. The population [residents of Willowbrook] has been among the earliest to have been vaccinated against measles and rubella, and soon shigellosis. Now the encouragement of promise against serum hepatitis.

The Study's Critics Missed the Big Picture

Yet are we faced with the conflict of truths. The ethical relativism, honest and honourable within the environment we are dedicated to serve, is questioned. The truth is that our conscience does not inhabit a germ-free area and the children were sick upon it. Our actions are dissected by words and the result is fatuous [silly].

We are physicians, dedicated to life, to support, to teach, to grow with our knowledge, to offer more because of this knowledge.

A farmer may pull up corn seedlings to destroy them, or he may pull them up to set them in hills for better growing. How then does one judge the deed without the motive?

We are advised to improve the situation; but of what is the situation but a child (and retarded at that), and a virus (whose only constancy is its love-affair with the human host), and society (who puts them together and departs). In our honesty we cannot separate the child from the situation of which he is an integral part: both cause and effect. To do so is a trick of words.

And what of knowledge? A physician brings to the care

of a patient all the knowledge of which he is possessed (much of it born of controversy now forgotten), and learns from each patient to whom he ministers. In our honesty, we have learned. We cannot separate knowledge from the child, no more than deed from motive, or child from situation.

And the word "experiment"? This is a word whose Latin origin (*experiri*) is the same as that of "experience" (*ex peritus*), the one infinitive, the other past participle, the latter not existing without the former. So much for words.

Each Must Obey His Conscience

Now examine the accusation that "infected material" is injected into children, and let us discuss knowledge, and *degree* of infectivity, and resultant gain. Yes gain, and to the child. For the half-truth of the accusation is that we proceed blind and wanton [cruel without limits] for our own unspeakable advantage. The thought shames us, for here is proof that you have never known us, that you have not come the three thousand miles to know what you condemn, nor walked with us even the first mile. For here is truth: you cannot clinically tell the newly admitted child from the child injected, at the height of response, from the child whose response is over, except for the fact that those who have been with us longer, by virtue of our care, are better adjusted, better nourished, and more scheduled within their capabilities. And immune, and this is a measurable fact. Your assumption is of illness. We have seen more reaction to countless vaccines than to the procedure we have so carefully controlled.

Truth is many things; the truth of parents, realistic after trial; the truth of critics, idealistic and apprehensive of what they have not seen and do not know; there is the truth of those whose judgment has led to action, and the truth, acknowledged, that there are no absolutes. There is the final truth that above all else man must help man, and the knowledge that each may approach by a different path, in conscience.

4

Parental Consent Does Not Justify Experimenting on Retarded Children

Stephen Goldby

In the following letter, British physician Stephen Goldby takes the editor of the medical journal the *Lancet* to task for lauding the work of Saul Krugman and his fellow researchers without ever considering that their hepatitis experiments at Willowbrook were unethical. Krugman had always defended the Willowbrook research by pointing out that it adhered to international ethics codes governing human experimentation by involving only those students whose parents had offered consent. Goldby argues that the international ethics code is in fact flawed. He maintains that it is never right to perform experiments on children that will harm rather than benefit them, whether parental consent is granted or not. The editor of the *Lancet* later agreed with Goldby and apologized for failing to confront the ethical questions raised by the Willowbrook study.

Y ou [referring to the editor] have referred to the work of Krugman and his colleagues at the Willowbrook State School in three editorials. In the first article the work was cited as a notable study of hepatitis and a model for this type of investigation. No comment was made on the rightness of attempting to infect mentally retarded children with hepati-

Stephen Goldby, "Experiments at the Willowbrook State School," *The Lancet*, vol. 1, April 10, 1971. Copyright © 1971 by The Lancet Ltd. Reproduced with permission from Elsevier.

tis for experimental purposes, in an institution where the disease was already endemic.

The second editorial again did not remark on the ethics of the study, but the third sounded a note of doubt as to the justification for extending these experiments. The reason given was that some children might have been made more susceptible to serious hepatitis as the result of the administration of previously heated icterogenic [related to jaundice] material.

Is it right to perform an experiment on a normal or mentally retarded child when no benefit can result to that individual? I think that the answer is no.

I believe that not only this last experiment, but the whole of Krugman's study, is quite unjustifiable, whatever the aims, and however academically or therapeutically important are the results. I am amazed that the work was published and that it has been actively supported editorially by the *Journal of the American Medical Association* and by . . . the 1967–68 *Year Book of Medicine*. To my knowledge only the *British Journal of Hospital Medicine* has clearly stated the ethical position on these experiments and shown that it was indefensible to give potentially dangerous infected material to children, particularly those who were mentally retarded, with or without parental consent, when no benefit to the child could conceivably result.

Krugman and [J.P.] Giles have continued to publish the results of their study, and in a recent paper go to some length to describe their method of obtaining parental consent and list a number of influential medical boards and committees that have approved the study. They point out again that, in their opinion, their work conforms to the World Medical Association Draft Code of Ethics on Human Experimentation. They also say that hepatitis is still highly endemic in the school.

The Ends Do Not Justify the Means

This attempted defence is irrelevant to the central issue. Is it right to perform an experiment on a normal or mentally retarded child when no benefit can result to that individual? I think that the answer is no, and that the question of parental consent is irrelevant. In my view the studies of Krugman serve only to show that there is a serious loophole in the Draft Code, which under General Principles and Definitions puts the onus [responsibility] of consent for experimentation on children on the parent or guardian. It is this section that is quoted by Krugman. I would class his work as "experiments conducted solely for the acquisition of knowledge", under which heading the code states that "Persons retained in mental hospital or hospitals for mental defectives should not be used for human experiment". Krugman may believe that his experiments were for the benefit of his patients, meaning the individual patients used in the study. If this is his belief he has a difficult case to defend. The duty of a pædiatrician in a situation such as exists at Willowbrook State School is to attempt to improve that situation, not to turn it to his advantage for experimental purposes, however lofty the aims.

Every new reference to the work of Krugman and Giles adds to its apparent ethical respectability, and in my view such references should stop, or at least be heavily qualified. The editorial attitude of *The Lancet* to the work should be reviewed and openly stated. The issue is too important to be ignored.

If Krugman and Giles are keen to continue their experiments I suggest that they invite the parents of the children involved to participate. I wonder what the response would be.

5

A Willowbrook Researcher Defends the Project

Saul Krugman

Fifteen years after the Willowbrook hepatitis study ended, its chief epidemiologist, Saul Krugman, still felt compelled to clarify the study's purpose and to offer a spirited defense of himself and his colleagues, all of whom had been accused of unethical medical research. In the following article he argues that rather than taking advantage of the mentally retarded Willowbrook participants, as their detractors had accused them, he and his fellow researchers had helped the children develop immunity against a virus they would have inevitably contracted simply by living at Willowbrook. Krugman further suggests that society and its failure to deal with institutional overcrowding were to blame for the hepatitis problem at the school. He states that he and his colleagues were simply trying to better understand and control the disease.

During the first half of this century, outbreaks of various infectious diseases were prevalent in orphanages, military barracks, and institutions for mentally retarded children. These outbreaks involved highly susceptible populations living in conditions of overcrowding and poor hygiene. Certain infectious diseases, such as influenza and measles, occurred as epidemics at variable intervals. Other infections, such as shigellosis and hepatitis, were generally endemic in nature.

Saul Krugman, "The Willowbrook Hepatitis Studies Revisited: Ethical Aspects," *Reviews of Infectious Diseases*, vol.8, January/February 1986. Copyright © 1986 by The University of Chicago. All rights reserved. Reproduced by permission.

During the mid-1950s my colleague, Dr. Robert Ward, and I were invited to join the staff of Willowbrook State School as consultants in infectious diseases. This institution for mentally retarded children had been plagued by the occurrence of such epidemic and endemic diseases as measles and hepatitis. Our efforts during the next two decades were devoted to the control of these infectious diseases.

In 1960 an epidemic of measles swept through Willowbrook, leaving 60 children dead. The studies that we initiated with the live attenuated [reduced] measles vaccine developed by Dr. John Enders and his colleagues culminated in the eradication of measles from the institution by the end of 1963.

Hepatitis, which affected virtually every child in Willowbrook as well as many employees, proved to be a more difficult problem. It was essential to acquire new knowledge about the natural history of this disease—knowledge that might lead to its ultimate control.

Krugman Argues Studies Were Ethical

The studies during the subsequent two decades were perceived by some critics to be unethical. As a matter of fact, in recent years the name "Willowbrook" has become synonymous with medical research gone astray. With time, facts have become distorted or forgotten, leaving only emotions.

Thirty years have elapsed since the Willowbrook hepatitis studies were initiated in the mid-1950s. I am as convinced today as I was at that time that our studies were ethical and justifiable. This judgement is based on knowledge of the extraordinary conditions that existed in the institution as well as on an assessment of the potential risks and benefits for the participants. The purpose of this article is to discuss the ethical aspects of our studies, within their appropriate historical context. It is hoped that this information will enable the reader to make an independent, objective judgement as to the ethics of the Willowbrook studies.

Willowbrook Had a History of Overcrowding

In 1938 the New York state legislature perceived the need for an additional institution for the care of mentally retarded children. It allocated funds to purchase 375 acres of land located at Willowbrook on Staten Island and authorized the construction of facilities to care for 3,000 mentally retarded children from the greater–New York metropolitan area. The institution, completed in 1942 and designated Willowbrook State School, was taken over by the federal government to meet an urgent need for an army hospital to care for disabled military personnel from World War II. The U.S. Army Medical Corps renamed it the Halloran General Hospital in honor of the late Colonel Paul Stacey Halloran, a U.S. Army medical corpsman.

After the war ended in 1945, there was considerable political pressure to retain Halloran General Hospital as a Veterans Administration hospital. The conflict between the needs of the Veterans Administration and the needs of the New York State Department of Mental Hygiene was described in the following letter sent by Governor Thomas Dewey to General Omar Bradley, who was director of the Veterans Administration at that time.

> Every year in the State of New York, thousands of children come into this world who are mentally and physically defective and feeble minded, who never can become members of society. They require constant care, both medically and physically, and in many cases, for social, psychological and economic reasons, few parents can afford to place them in private institutions. Even if such institutions existed in sufficient quantity, the result is that the state must take responsibility for the care of these children and do so with a high degree of tenderness and attention.

> At present, the State of New York operates two downstate institutions for the care of such infants and children. One is the Wassaic State School in Duchess and the other is Letchworth Village in Rockland County. There are several other state schools for mental defectives but they are too overcrowded and none is or can be equipped for the additonal care of infants.

> Hundreds of infants and children unable to care for themselves are sleeping on mattresses on floors of these institutions. What is more serious is that there are eight to nine hundred infants on the waiting list for admission and the State Commission of Mental Hygiene daily must deal with distracted parents who seek to have their children placed in state institutions. The mail of the

Commissioner of Mental Hygiene is filled with letters from such parents, many of whom are veterans.

It seems to me that we are now confronted with these two conflicting obligations at Willowbrook. The first is that of the Federal Government to provide hospital care for its veterans after they are discharged from service. The second is the obligation of the State of New York to provide care for permanently helpless infants. Obviously, Willowbrook cannot be used for both.

Finally, on October 24, 1947, after a delay of five years, 10 patients from Wassaic State School and 10 patients from Letchworth Village were transferred to Willowbrook State School. Initially, patients were both transferred from other institutions and admitted from the community. In retrospect, it is apparent that the infectious diseases endemic in Wassaic State School and Letchworth Village were introduced into Willowbrook by patients who were transferred from these institutions.

Overcrowding Led to Disease

The occurrence of so-called infectious hepatitis was first observed in 1949. Later, in response to extraordinary pressure from many parents, the patient population increased rapidly in subsequent years; it exceeded 3,000 in 1953, 4,000 in 1955, and eventually it exceeded 6,000. In his report to a joint legislative committee on mental and physical handicap, the late Dr. Jack Hammond, director of Willowbrook State School stated:

> The overcrowded conditions in the buildings make care, treatment, supervision and possible training of the patients difficult, if not impossible. When the patients are up and in the day rooms, they are crowded together, soiling, attacking each other, abusing themselves and destroying their clothing. At night in many of the dormitories the beds must be placed together in order to provide sufficient space for all patients. Therefore, except for one narrow aisle, it is virtually necessary to climb over beds in order to reach the children.

The residents of Willowbrook State School were the most severely retarded, the most handicapped, and the most helpless of those being cared for in the New York state system. The population of about 6,000 included 77% who were severely or profoundly retarded, 60% who were not toilet trained, 39% who were not ambulatory, 30% who had convulsive seizures, and 64% who were incapable of feeding themselves. Thus, the conditions were optimal for the transmission of hepatitis, shigellosis, respiratory infections, and parasitic infections.

We were not qualified to deal with the societal problems, but we believed that we could help control the existing medical problem of hepatitis.

By the early 1950s the director of Willowbrook and his staff were convinced that serious overcrowding and an inadequate staff were in great part responsible for the increasing hepatitis problem. Their statistics indicated that the annual attack rate of hepatitis with jaundice was 25 per 1,000 among the children and 40 per 1,000 among the adults. Efforts to correct this intolerable situation were unsuccessful. Society had created a problem, but it provided no solution. It was during that period that my colleague, the late Dr. Robert Ward, and I were asked to join the staff of Willowbrook as consultants in infectious diseases. We were not qualified to deal with the societal problems, but we believed that we could help control the existing medical problem of hepatitis.

Hepatitis Survey Reveals an Epidemic

Our first objective in 1955 was to carry out an extensive epidemiologic survey. We were fortunate because new tests to detect hepatic dysfunction were described that year, namely, serum glutamic oxaloacetic transaminase (SGOT) and serum glutamic pyruvic transaminase (SGPT). These sensitive assays [tests] enabled us to detect the presence of hepatitis without jaundice (anicteric hepatitis). Today, SGOT is called alanine aspartate transaminase (AST), and SGPT is called alanine aminotransferase (ALT).

Our colleague, the late Dr. Joan P. Giles, joined us during this period. During the course of our epidemiologic surveys and the performance of routine physical examinations, she collected many thousands of serum specimens. Instead of discarding them—the usual practice in most laboratories—we stored them in an increasing number of deep freezers. The scientific dividends of this serum bank proved to be incalculable in later years.

After the results of the SGOT and SGPT assays were reviewed, it was obvious that the detected cases of icteric hepatitis represented the tip of a hepatitis iceberg. The results of these highly sensitive tests of liver dysfunction convinced us that most newly admitted children were destined to contract hepatitis infection under the conditions that existed in the institution. The occurrence of hepatitis among Willowbrook children was as predictable and inevitable as the occurrence of respiratory inflections among children in day care centers.

During the course of our epidemiologic survey in 1955, all of the evidence indicated that the endemic disease was so-called infectious or type A hepatitis, an infection that spread via the fecal-oral route [feces to mouth]. The disease was mild and there were no deaths. Although the same disease was more severe and more debilitating in the adult employees, they, too, recovered completely. Previous experience of various investigators had revealed that hepatitis A was much milder in children than in adults. Efforts to reduce the overcrowded conditions at Willowbrook continued to be unsuccessful. In a desperate attempt the director mailed letters to about 5,000 parents, requesting that they return a questionnaire that contained the statement, "I wish to discuss the possibility and advisability of removing my child from Willowbrook State School so that he/she can live at home." A total of 24 parents responded, and only two children were taken home at that time!

The Parameters for the Study

After one year of careful observation and study in 1955, we concluded that the control of hepatitis in Willowbrook could be achieved if it were possible to devise and conduct well-designed studies to shed new light on the natural history and prevention of the disease—new knowledge that could conceivably lead to the development of a vaccine. Thus, our decision to propose the exposure of a small number of newly admitted children to the endemic Willowbrook strain of hepatitis virus was reached after serious consideration of the following factors and assumptions:

(1) As indicated previously, under the conditions exist-

ing in the institution, most newly admitted children would
contract hepatitis. This empiric impression was confirmed
in the 1970s when newly developed serologic tests revealed
that >90% of the residents of the institution had hepatitis A
and B markers of past infection.

(2) Hepatitis was known to be especially mild in the
three- to 10-year age group that would participate in the
studies. Our extensive survey confirmed that most infections were inapparent or benign [non–life threatening] and
there were no deaths.

(3) The artificially induced infection would induce immunity to the endemic strain of hepatitis virus and, we
hoped, to other strains that might be introduced by new admissions or transfers to Willowbrook. Studies in the 1940s
had revealed that hepatitis A infection was followed by ho-
mologous [genetically similar] immunity. Therefore, the artificially induced infection would be prophylactic [prevent-
ing further infection].

(4) The children would be admitted to a specially
equipped, specially staffed unit where they would be isolated from exposure to other endemic infectious diseases occurring in the institution—namely, shigellosis, respiratory
infections, and parasitic infections.

(5) Only children whose parents gave consent would be
included. Our method of obtaining informed consent
changed progressively during the course of the studies. In
1956 the information was conveyed to individual parents by
letter or personal interview. Later, we adopted a group tech-
nique of obtaining consent. First, a psychiatric social worker
discussed the project with parents during a preliminary interview. Those who were interested were invited to attend a
group session at the institution to discuss the project in
greater detail. These sessions were conducted by our staff
responsible for the program, including Dr. Giles, the super-
vising nurse, staff attendants, and psychiatric social workers.
Meetings were often attended by outside physicians who
had expressed interest. Parents, in groups of six to eight,
were given a tour of the facilities. The purposes, potential
benefits, and potential hazards of the program were discussed with them, and they were encouraged to ask questions. Thus, all parents could hear the response to questions
posed by the more articulate members of the group. After
leaving this briefing session, parents had an opportunity to

talk with their private physicians, who could call Dr. Giles for more information. Approximately two weeks after the visit, the psychiatric social worker contacted the parents for their decision. If the decision was in the affirmative, the consent was signed, but parents were informed that consent could be withdrawn at any time. It was clear that the group method enabled us to obtain a more thorough informed consent. Children who were wards of the state or children without parents were never included in our studies.

From 1956 the protocols were reviewed and sanctioned by various local, state, and federal agencies. These studies were reviewed and approved by the New York University and Willowbrook State School committees on human experimentation after their formation in February 1967. Prior to this date, the functions of the present Institutional Review Board were performed by the Executive Faculty of the School of Medicine for studies of this type. The initial proposal in 1956 was reviewed and approved by the following groups: Executive Faculty, New York University School of Medicine; New York State Department of Mental Hygiene; New York State Department of Health; and Armed Forces Epidemiological Board. It is of interest that the guidelines that were adopted for the hepatitis studies at their inception in 1956 conformed to the World Medical Association's draft Code of Ethics on Human Experimentation, which was presented to its general assembly in September 1961, five years later. It is also of interest that our established policy of informed consent was instituted at least 10 years before it was mandated by most research institutes and medical centers in the United States.

Willowbrook Residents Were Destined to Get Hepatitis

During the period 1956–1967, we believed that we were dealing with endemicity [localization] of hepatitis A, an infection that should be followed by lasting immunity. However, by 1967 it was obvious that many children had had two attacks of hepatitis. Our studies of this phenomenon revealed that one attack was caused by the so-called MS-1 strain of hepatitis virus and the second attack, by the MS-2 strain. Thus, it became apparent that two types of hepatitis were endemic in Wiliowbrook—MS-1, resembling hepatitis A, and MS-2, resembling hepatitis B. By 1969, after

[Dr. Baruch] Blumberg discovered the Australia antigen, the new technology enabled us to confirm that Willow-brook MS-2 serum contained hepatitis B antigen.

The fact that the children were mentally retarded was relevant only to the extent that society placed them in an institution where hepatitis was prevalent.

Our serum bank contained specimens obtained from most patients who contracted naturally acquired hepatitis during the period 1956–1969. When we tested these serum specimens in the 1970s, using the newly developed serologic [serum-based] assays, it was obvious that both hepatitis A (MS-1) and hepatitis B (MS-2) had been endemic in the institution since 1956. It was also apparent that hepatitis B, like hepatitis A, was generally a mild or inapparent infection in Willowbrook children. . . . During the course of [a] new survey, we found that most children had markers of present or past hepatitis B infection. Thus, it was likely that newly admitted children would be intensely exposed to both types of hepatitis. When this new information was presented to the members of the Commission on Viral Infections of the Armed Forces Epidemiological Board in 1969, they agreed that the studies should be continued.

It should be emphasized that the studies were conducted in Willowbrook State School because hepatitis was a severe problem in this institution and not, as some charged, because we were looking for a facile [easily used] "guinea pig" population. The fact that the children were mentally retarded was relevant only to the extent that society placed them in an institution where hepatitis was prevalent. The primary objective of our studies was to protect the children and employees while acquiring new knowledge in the process.

The accomplishments of the Willowbrook studies are well documented in the medical literature. . . .

Studies Benefited Residents

While I agree with the critics of medical research who state that the ends (successful accomplishments) do not justify the means, I believe that this generalization does not apply to our Willowbrook studies. Under the conditions that existed in the institution, all children were constantly exposed to the naturally acquired hepatitis viruses. Moreover, the overall risk for children in our special isolation unit was less than the risk for other children who were admitted to buildings in the institution where shigellosis and respiratory infections, as well as hepatitis, were endemic.

A century ago [French physiologist] Claude Bernard defined the limits of human experimentation. He stated that

> it is our duty and our right to perform an experiment on man whenever it can save life, cure him, or gain some potential benefit. The principle of medical and surgical morality, therefore, consists in never performing on man an experiment which might be harmful to him to any extent, even though the result may be highly advantageous to science or to the health of others. But performing experiments and operations exclusively from the point of view of the patient's own advantage does not prevent their turning out profitably to science.

My colleague, the late Dr. Joan P. Giles, expressed it beautifully and succinctly in her letter to the *Lancet* [a medical journal] published May 29, 1971, in which she said, "A farmer may pull up corn seedlings to destroy them or he may pull them up to set them in better hills for better growing. How then does one judge the deed without the motive?" This describes the motivation for our studies at Willowbrook State School.

Many Supported Krugman's Work

I am greatly indebted to many collaborators, colleagues, and organizations for support and encouragement during the course of our Willowbrook hepatitis studies:

To the late Dr. Robert Ward, who was the principal investigator of our studies from 1956 to 1958. He was an outstanding investigator and a colleague who had exceptional human qualities.

To the late Dr. Joan P. Giles, who died of cancer in 1973 after devoting 17 years of her life to the care of the children in our hepatitis unit. She was a highly ethical physician and a person of great humanity and integrity.

To Harriet Friedman and Cass Lattimer, research associates, for more than 25 years of competent and meticulous work in our laboratory.

To the late Dr. Jack Hammond, director of Willowbrook State School. He and his dedicated staff labored under the most difficult circumstances. They were subjected to incredible abuse by certain representatives of the news media and by publicity-seeking legislators who criticized them for the horrible conditions in the institution. Their morale was devastated because they knew that the pressures of society (distraught parents and their legislators) were responsible for increasing the census to more than 6,000 in a 3,000-bed institution. It was "society" that was responsible for the overcrowded, unhygienic conditions in Willowbrook, not the dedicated people who worked there under stressful conditions.

To the late Dr. John R. Paul and Dr. Robert McCollum of Yale University for their encouragement and wise counsel during the 1950s and 1960s.

To the Armed Forces Epidemiological Board and the U.S. Army Medical Research and Development Command for 25 consecutive years of financial support.

And, finally, to many loyal and devoted colleagues and friends whose support helped ease the pain inflicted by many vicious attacks during the late 1960s and early 1970s. We were especially grateful to the parents of the Willowbrook chapter of the Benevolent Society of Retarded Children for the plaque that they presented to us at their 1967 annual meeting. The inscription on the plaque stated, "In recognition of distinguished, pioneering, humanitarian research in the prevention of infectious diseases and their resultant complication in children, born and unborn."

6

Saul Krugman Endangered Children for the Sake of His Research Interests

David J. Rothman and Sheila M. Rothman

In their book *The Willowbrook Wars*, public affairs writers David J. Rothman and Sheila M. Rothman describe the head Willowbrook hepatitis researcher, Saul Krugman, as an ambitious man who cared more about discovering a vaccine for hepatitis than the children he experimented on. Krugman's main defense of the Willowbrook hepatitis study was that it was not unethical to observe the progress of the disease since there was no known treatment for it. The Rothmans point out, however, that deliberately infecting children with live hepatitis virus so that he and fellow researchers could continue their experiments went beyond observation and was immoral. Further, they argue, had Krugman held the high standards for medical ethics that he claimed governed his research, he would have tried to address the conditions at Willowbrook that contributed to the spread of the disease, such as overcrowding and poor hygiene practices. Instead, he conducted experiments that further propogated the hepatitis virus. In addition to the book he wrote with his wife Sheila, David Rothman has written *Strangers at the Bedside: A History of How Law and Bioethics Transformed Medical Decision Making* and *Beginnings Count: The Technological Imperative in American Health Care.*

The attempt to bar Willowbrook's hepatitis carriers from the public schools had a special irony to it, for from 1956 through 1971, researchers fed live viruses to children in Willowbrook in order to study the disease and attempt to create a vaccine against it.

The head of the team was Saul Krugman. In appearance, he borders on the colorless, but controversy surrounds him. Krugman's research at Willowbrook brought him fame and power. He has chaired national committees on hepatitis, directed huge federally funded projects, been the subject of laudatory editorials in the *Journal of the American Medical Association*, and won the John Russell Award of the Markle Foundation (which read, in part: "In all his work Dr. Krugman proceeded quietly and cautiously. . . . He has zealously guarded the rights and sensibilities of patients and their families. . . . Dr. Krugman has provided an example of how [good clinical research] should be done"). Yet in April 1972, when Dr. Krugman received a prize from the American College of Physicians, a line of police surrounded the podium while 150 protesters denounced his research as grossly unethical.

If Willowbrook was a hell for its residents, it could be a paradise for a reseacher.

Saul Krugman's interest in infectious diseases began when, as a physician with the armed forces in the South Pacific, he treated many patients who contracted malaria or jungle parasites. Upon discharge, Krugman took a residency at New York's public hospital for infectious diseases, Willard Parker, which in several ways prepared him to work at Willowbrook. Krugman recalled entering a pavilion where some sixty children lay one next to the other "with every complication of measles—encephalitis, pneumonia, everything. I could go to another area and see dozens of children with diphtheria. . . . Every summer the Parker Hospital would admit at least 50 and sometimes more than 100 children with paralytic poliomyelitis."

In such a setting, Krugman became convinced that even the most diligent efforts at treatment were not likely to bring benefits. "Therapeutics," he once remarked, "was a slender reed in those days." Rather, the goal had to be prevention, which to Krugman meant not cleaning up a water supply or sewer system, but finding vaccines.

Willowbrook Provided Many Research Opportunities

In 1947, Krugman moved to Bellevue Hospital and joined the NYU faculty, and in 1954 he became consulting physician to the newly opened Willowbrook facility. He immediately conducted an epidemiological survey, which disclosed an amazing variety of infectious diseases: measles, hepatitis, respiratory infections, shigella, and assorted intestinal parasites.

If Willowbrook was a hell for its residents, it could be a paradise for a researcher. On these disease-ridden wards, the line between treatment and experimentation seemed to vanish. A researcher could select his disease and enjoy substantial freedom to experiment, believing that he was serving both society and the residents.

But how could feeding live hepatitis viruses to children be considered the equivalent of observing a disease?

Events in 1960 confirmed the validity of these presumptions for Krugman. Every two years or so, New York City experienced a measles epidemic, and new admissions to Willowbrook invariably brought in the disease. The results were usually disastrous, with hundreds of cases and fatality rates as high as 10 percent. At the start of 1960, Dr. John Enders, working in Boston, had succeeded in growing measles virus in culture and had managed to attenuate [thin] it to the point where it might be an effective vaccine. Krugman wanted to run trial tests at Willowbrook. The disease struck there so often and so hard that findings could be obtained quickly; and if the vaccine offered protection, the Willowbrook residents would obviously benefit. Krugman contacted Enders, received twenty samples of the limited number of doses available, and vaccinated the residents of one ward.

A measles epidemic soon struck at Willowbrook, but no one among the vaccinated children contracted the disease. "Willowbrook's children," observed Dr. Krugman, "enabled us to acquire in a short time solid information about Dr. Enders's vaccine." By 1963, before the vaccine was officially licensed, 90 percent of Willowbrook's residents had been inoculated, and measles was never again a threat. The use of an experimental vaccine at Willowbrook, Krugman concluded, "was obviously beneficial to the children."

Krugman Wanted to Solve Hepatitis Riddle

The measles study was a sideshow at Willowbrook. It was hepatitis that held center stage. Soon after completing his initial epidemiological survey, Dr. Krugman decided to explore this widespread but little understood disease. Its symptoms had been recognized for centuries, but not until World War II did medical researchers suspect that the disease was infectious and occurred in two varieties: the short, thirty-day-incubation type that we now label hepatitis A and commonly associate with eating contaminated shellfish; and the long, ninety-day-incubation type that we now label hepatitis B and commonly associate with blood transfusions. Beyond these simple categories, little was known about causes, cure, or prevention.

In this vacuum Dr. Krugman began his experiments. Between 1953 and 1957, Willowbrook had had about 350 cases of hepatitis among the residents and 76 among the staff; in 1955 alone (the year before his research began), the disease rate was 25 per thousand among the residents, 40 per thousand among the staff. (In New York State, the rate was 25 per *one hundred thousand* of the population.) And these figures included only the observable, acute cases of patients with jaundice; the number of milder, subclinical cases was still greater. To Dr. Krugman, these conditions called for an active research strategy. Scientists had not yet found a nonhuman host for the virus or succeeded in growing it in a laboratory culture. Thus experiments would have to be carried out on live subjects, and what better subjects than the Willowbrook children? The high rate of contagion in the institution meant that they were bound to get the disease and the effectiveness of intervention could be measured almost immediately.

Krugman's experiments had a logic, a simplicity, and, one would dare to add, an elegance about them. His initial project was to determine whether injections of gamma globulin, that part of the blood plasma which is rich in antibodies, protected recipients against hepatitis. The literature suggested that gamma globulin offered temporary, "passive" immunity; the antibodies in the fluid would be able to counteract the disease for some six weeks. The critical question was whether injections of gamma globulin in the presence of the virus would lead recipients to produce their own antibodies, thereby acquiring permanent immunity that would last for years.

Experiments with Gamma Globulin

The team first administered varying doses of gamma globulin to one group of new admissions to Willowbrook and withheld it from another. Then, eight to ten months later, it tallied the numbers from each group who had contracted the illness. The results were clear: of 1,812 residents who had been inoculated, only two cases of hepatitis occurred (a rate of 1.7 per 1,000); of the 1,771 residents who were not inoculated, forty-one contracted the disease (22.5 per 1,000). Thus Krugman confirmed that gamma globulin did protect against hepatitis and the finding "pointed the way to the practical method for the control of infectious hepatitis at this institution."

But had the gamma globulin injection stimulated active immunity? Those inoculated were protected against the disease for almost a year, but no one understood how this protection was acquired or how long it would last. Had the gamma globulin first provided a passive immunity, which then turned active when recipients came in contact with the live virus from other residents? Could permanent active immunity be acquired by injecting patients with gamma globulin and live virus at the same time?

To answer these questions, Krugman opened a separate unit on the Willowbrook grounds. Staffed by its own personnel, it admitted children between the ages of three and eleven, directly from their own homes; when their role in the research was completed, weeks or months later, they moved onto the general wards. The experiments typically involved injecting some of the unit residents with gamma globulin and feeding them the live hepatitis virus (obtained from the feces of Willowbrook hepatitis patients). At the same time, other unit residents served as "controls"; they were fed the live virus without the benefit of gamma globulin, to ascertain that the virus was actually "live," capable of transmitting the disease, and to measure the different responses. Then Krugman would calculate how many of those who had received both gamma globulin and live virus, as compared with controls, initially came down with hepatitis; six or nine or twelve months later, he would again feed both groups another dose of live virus and measure how many of those who had earlier received the gamma globulin contracted the disease as against those who had not.

When overcrowding at Willowbrook forced a close in regular admissions, an escape hatch was left—admission via Krugman's unit.

As is often the case in scientific research, Dr. Krugman's most important observation came by chance. In keeping track of the hepatitis rates in the institution, he noted that 4 to 8 percent of those who contracted hepatitis went on to suffer a second attack within a year. The second attack might possibly have been caused by a very heavy exposure to the virus, which overwhelmed the immunity the body had built up after the first attack. But Dr. Krugman believed that the etiology [cause] of the disease was more complicated than researchers had recognized. The repeat attack indicated that more than one type of virus could be causing hepatitis.

Krugman Discerns Two Hepatitis Viruses

To investigate this "very attractive hypothesis," Dr. Krugman in 1964 started a new series of experiments, and within three years he helped to clarify the distinction between hepatitis A and B. In this round, the Krugman team admitted new Willowbrook residents to its special unit and fed them a dose of pooled Willowbrook virus, that is, a mixture that came from a large number of hepatitis victims and, therefore, contained all the hepatitis viruses within the institution. In short order, these First Trial subjects contracted the disease and recovered from it. The team then reinfected these children with the same pooled virus in a Second Trial, and a number of them again contracted the disease. In the course of these procedures, the team drew a sample of blood from one of the boys during his first illness (and labeled it MS-1), and then another sample from him in his second illness (labeled MS-2). Next, the researchers admitted a new group of fourteen children to the unit and infected these Third Trial subjects with the MS-1 virus. Within thirty-one to thirty-eight days, all but one came down with hepatitis. Simultaneously, the team admitted still another fourteen children to the unit, and injected this Fourth Trial group with the MS-2 virus. Within forty-one to sixty-nine days, all but two contracted the illness. Now the stage was set for the final procedure. The team gave all the hepatitis victims in the third (MS-1) group and fourth (MS-2) group the MS-1 virus. It turned out that not one child in the Third Trial group came down with hepatitis a second time; six of the eight children in the Fourth Trial group again contracted the disease.

With these findings in hand, Krugman announced that hepatitis was caused by at least two distinct viruses. There was hepatitis A, MS-1, of short incubation and highly contagious (all of the controls who lived with the Third Trial group but were not fed the virus directly came down with the disease). And there was hepatitis B, MS-2, of long incubation and lower contagion (only two of the five controls living with the Fourth Trial group caught the disease). In short, the Krugman research established the distinctive features of two strains of hepatitis.

Krugman Praised for His Ethics

The findings met with acclaim, and Krugman was praised not only for his results but for his methods. The *Journal of the American Medical Association* credited Krugman's "judicious use of human beings"; Franz Inglefinger, later the editor of the *New England Journal of Medicine*, went further: "By being allowed to participate in a carefully supervised study and by receiving the most expert attention available for a disease of basically unknown nature, the patients themselves benefited. . . . How much better to have a patient with hepatitis, accidentally or deliberately acquired, under the guidance of a Krugman than under the care of a [rights-minded] zealot."

Underlying these attempts at justification, and those that Krugman himself made, was the notion that the Willowbrook experiments were, in the words of Claude Bernard, the nineteenth-century French physician who was among the first to address the ethics of research, "experiments in nature." Researchers who studied the course and spread of a disease that had no known antidote were acting ethically, for no intervention on their part could have altered the outcome. But how could feeding live hepatitis viruses to children be considered the equivalent of observing a disease? Krugman's answer was that if he had not infected the children, they still would have contracted hepatitis. Had he never come to Willowbrook, the likelihood was overwhelming that entering residents would have suffered the disease. Thus his feeding them the virus did not really change anything and was an experiment in nature. Krugman also noted that he had obtained permission from the parents of all his subjects, and he had signed consent forms to prove it.

Many parents of children accepted at Willowbrook but still awaiting actual admission—a wait that could last for several years—did receive the following letter from Dr. H.H. Berman, then Willowbrook's director:

November 15, 1958

Dear Mrs. _____ :

We are studying the possibility of preventing epidemics of hepatitis on a new principle. Virus is introduced and gamma globulin given later to some, so that either no attack or only a mild attack of hepatitis is expected to follow. This may give the children immunity against this disease for life. We should like to give your child this new form of prevention with the hope that it will afford protection.

Permission form is enclosed for your consideration. If you wish to have your child given the benefit of this new preventive, will you so signify by signing the form.

The Letter to Parents Was Misleading

Almost every phrase in this particular letter encourages parents to commit their children to the unit. The team is "studying" hepatitis, not doing research. The virus "is introduced," in the passive voice, rather than the team's being said to feed the child a live virus. Gamma globulin is given "to some," but the letter does not explicitly state that it is withheld from others. "No attack" or a "mild attack" of the disease "is expected to follow," but absent gamma globulin, a claim of "no attack" was false and left unsaid was that in some cases the attack would not be mild. Finally, the letter twice described introducing the live virus as a "new form of prevention," but feeding a child hepatitis hardly amounted to prevention. In truth, the goal of the experiment was to *create*, not deliver, a new form of protection.

To send such a letter over the signature of Willowbrook's director appeared coercive. These parents wanted to please the man who would be in charge of their child. Moreover, an especially raw form of coercion may have occasionally intruded. When overcrowding at Willowbrook forced a close in regular admissions, an escape hatch was left—admission via Krugman's unit. A parent wanting to institutionalize a retarded child had a choice: Sign the form or forgo the placement.

Krugman Endangered Children's Health

What of Krugman's contention that his research was an experiment in nature? The claim ignores the fact that the underlying problem was not ignorance about a disease but an unwillingness to alter the social environment. Had Krugman wished to, he could have insisted that hygienic measures be introduced to decrease the spread of the virus. Should the facility resist carrying out the necessary cleanup, he might have asked the Department of Health to close the place down as a health hazard, which it surely was. Furthermore, Krugman had at hand an antidote of some efficacy. His own findings demonstrated that gamma globulin provided some protection, and yet he infected control groups with the virus and withheld the serum from them in order to fulfill the requirements of his research design.

Finally, to introduce one more irony to this account: While Krugman was trying to discover the etiology of hepatitis at Willowbrook, Dr. Baruch Blumberg was actually solving the puzzle in his laboratory, without conducting experiments on humans. In the course of his research on the body's immunological reaction to transfused blood, Blumberg observed that a strange band occurred when he mixed a vial of blood drawn from a hemophiliac with that drawn from an Australian aborigine. Labeling the band the Australia antigen, he investigated its properties; like a detective on the trail of a culprit, he followed several false leads and then the true one, discovering that the Australia antigen was the infective agent in hepatitis B. His first published report appeared in 1967 and Krugman confirmed the finding (the Australia antigen was in the blood of the MS-2 children but not the MS-1 children). Thus those with a utilitarian bent, who might be prepared to give Krugman leeway with his means because his ends were important, will have to consider that, however accidentally, we would have learned almost everything we needed to know about hepatitis B in the laboratory.

Chapter 3

The Fernald School Radiation Experiments

1

The Fernald School Experiments Yield Important Nutritional Information

Felix Bronner et al.

Many prestigious medical researchers were involved with the nutrition studies at the Fernald school in Waltham, Massachusetts. Primary researcher Felix Bronner was a doctoral student at the Department of Food Technology at the Massachusetts Institute of Technology (MIT), where he received research funding for the radiated calcium study from the Quaker Oats Company. Robert S. Harris was employed by MIT's Department of Food Technology. Constantine J. Maletskos taught physics at MIT, and Clemens E. Benda was a member of the Department of Neuropsychiatry at Harvard Medical School and a physician and medical researcher at the Fernald school. In the following article, these four researchers describe their experiments at the Fernald school. They thank the boys, whom they describe as of "inadequate intelligence," for their participation in studies that yielded important information about the effect of cereals on calcium absorption. Bronner and his colleagues do not address the methods used to encourage study participation—methods that many consider unethical.

In the present investigation the effect of a phytate-rich [rich in plant matter] cereal (oatmeal) on the uptake of

Felix Bronner, Robert S. Harris, Constantine J. Maletskos, and Clemens E. Benda, "Studies in Calcium Metabolism: Effect of Food Phytates on Calcium Uptake in Children on Low-Calcium Breakfasts," *The Journal of Nutrition*, vol. 54, December 10, 1954, p. 524.

calcium was compared with that of a phytate-free cereal (farina). Milk, commonly taken in conjunction with cooked breakfast cereals, was used as the principal source of calcium. The effect of food phytates was further compared with that of soluble sodium phytate which was added to farina. In order to neutralize any effect due to the solids content of the food, all meals were equalized to a common solids content by the addition of farina.

The general procedure was to mix the radiocalcium [radioactive calcium] intimately with the milk of the test meal and then to measure the calcium and radiocalcium content of the serum, urine and feces at intervals following ingestion of the test meal of which the milk was a part.

A criss-cross design was used, that is, all individuals were given two test meals three weeks apart, to permit both paired and group comparisons. A three-week interval was chosen because preliminary studies had indicated that with an intake of 0.85 µc Ca^{45} the level of radiocalcium in blood, urine and feces was negligible after that time. This finding was again confirmed in these studies.

Nineteen adolescent boys, of inadequate intelligence but otherwise normal, who were institutionalized in a state school under uniform nutritional and environmental conditions, volunteered for these experiments.

Nineteen adolescent boys, of inadequate intelligence but otherwise normal, who were institutionalized in a state school under uniform nutritional and environmental conditions, volunteered for these experiments. The subjects were prepared for the study by giving each a daily supplement of one quart of milk and one multivitamin tablet during one month prior to the start of the experiment, and until it was concluded. . . .

It is interesting to note that the phytate naturally present in oatmeal is less reactive with food calcium than sodium phytate, since 78 mg of phytic phosphorus in the form of sodium phytate permitted much less calcium to be taken up than 116 mg of phytic phosphorus in the form of oat phytate (34 versus 55%).

The data presented would lead to the conclusion that less calcium was taken up when sodium phytate or when a phytate-containing cereal was fed than when the phytate-free farina was ingested. Taken together with the studies by earlier investigators ([R.A.] McCance and [E.M.] Widdowson, '49) these findings leave little room for doubt that phytate does interfere with calcium uptake, and that less calcium enters the body when phytate-containing cereals are eaten than when phytate-free cereals are ingested.

On the other hand, the absolute quantity of calcium rendered unavailable as a result of the action of the food phytate was so small (15 mg) that phytates cannot be very significant in the usual U.S. diets. . . .

1. Nineteen adolescent boys, of inadequate intelligence, but otherwise normal, who were institutionalized under uniform nutritional and other environmental conditions, were given three types of breakfast low in calcium: (I) oatmeal, (II) farina, and (III) farina and sodium phytate. These meals contained, respectively: 55, 60, and 60 ml of milk; 91, 83, and 83 mg of calcium; 116, 0, and 78 mg of phytic [plant-based] phosphorus, and 0.85, 0.85, and 0.85 µc of radioactive calcium (Ca^{45}). Calcium uptake was studied by measuring the Ca^{45} content of serum [watery component of blood], urine and feces for a period of 5 days. Individual variations were controlled by placing each subject on two different Ca^{45}-1abeled breakfasts, 30 days apart.

2. The uptake of Ca^{45} by the boys on the oatmeal breakfast was 74% as great as that of the boys on the farina breakfast. Similarly, the uptake of Ca^{45} by the boys on the farina plus phytate meal was 45% that of farina meal. These differences proved to be statistically significant on a 5% probability level.

3. Significantly less Ca^{45} was taken up in the presence of sodium phytate than in the presence of an equivalent quantity of phytic phosphorus supplied by oats.

2

The Fernald School Experiments Were Morally Wrong

Advisory Committee on Human Radiation Experiments

In 1994 the U.S. Department of Energy, led by Secretary Hazel O'Leary, convened the Advisory Committee on Human Radiation Experiments in an attempt to understand the role the United States had played in experiments conducted during the Cold War. A year later, the committee published a report of its findings in an effort to end years of secrecy and deception. The following section of the report details the committee's determination that the Fernald school experiments were morally wrong. As the report indicates, although the researchers provided consent forms to parents, they did not tell the parents that radioactive calcium would be part of their sons' "special diet." The report concludes that the Massachusetts Institute of Technology researchers and the federal agencies and the corporation that funded their research took advantage of a captive, helpless, and especially vulnerable group of children.

Researchers from the Massachusetts Institute of Technology, working in cooperation with senior members of the Fernald staff, carried out nontherapeutic nutritional studies with radioisotopes at the state school in the late 1940s and early 1950s. The subjects of these nutritional research studies were young male residents of Fernald, who were members of the school's "science club." In 1946, one study exposed sev-

Advisory Committee on Human Radiation Experiments, *Department of Energy Openness: Human Radiation Experiments: Roadmap to the Project*, February 1995.

enteen subjects to radioactive iron. The second study, which involved a series of seventeen related subexperiments, exposed fifty-seven subjects to radioactive calcium between 1950 and 1953. It is clear that the doses involved were low and that it is extremely unlikely that any of the children who were used as subjects were harmed as a consequence. These studies remain morally troubling, however, for several reasons. First, although parents or guardians were asked for their permission to have their children involved in the research, the available evidence suggests that the information provided was, at best, incomplete. Second, there is the question of the fairness of selecting institutionalized children at all, children whose life circumstances were by any standard already heavily burdened.

The researchers failed to satisfactorily inform the subjects and their families that the nutritional research studies were non-therapeutic.

The Massachusetts Task Force found two letters sent to parents describing the nutrition studies and seeking their permission. The first letter, a form letter signed by the superintendent of the school, is dated November 1949. The letter refers to a project in which children at the school will receive a special diet "rich" in various cereals, iron, and vitamins and for which "it will be necessary to make some blood tests at stated intervals, similar to those to which our patients are already accustomed, and which will cause no discomfort or change in their physical condition other than possibly improvement." The letter makes no mention of any risks or the use of a radioisotope. Parents or guardians are asked to indicate that they have no objection to their son's participation in the project by signing an enclosed form.

The second letter, dated May 1953, we quote in its entirety:

Dear Parent:

In previous years we have done some examinations in connection with the nutritional department of the Massachusetts Institute of Technology, with the purposes of helping to improve the nutrition of our children and to help them in general more efficiently than before.

For the checking up of the children, we occasionally need to take some blood samples, which are then analyzed. The blood samples are taken after one test meal which consists of a special breakfast meal containing a certain amount of calcium. We have asked for volunteers to give a sample of blood once a month for three months, and your son has agreed to volunteer because the boys who belong to the Science Club have many additional privileges. They get a quart of milk daily during that time, and are taken to a baseball game, to the beach and to some outside dinners and they enjoy it greatly.

I hope that you have no objection that your son is voluntarily participating in this study. The first study will start on Monday, June 8th, and if you have not expressed any objections we will assume that your son may participate.

Sincerely yours,

Clemens E. Benda, M.D.

[Fernald] Clinical Director

Approved: _____

Malcom J. Farrell, M.D.

[Fernald] Superintendent

Parents Were Not Adequately Informed

Again, there is no mention of any risks or the use of a radioisotope. It was believed then that the risks were minimal, as indeed they appear to have been, and as a consequence, school administrators and the investigators may have thought it unnecessary to raise the issue of risks with the parents. There was *no basis*, however, for the implication in both letters that the project was intended for the children's benefit or improvement. This was simply not true.

The conclusion of the Massachusetts Task Force was that these experiments were conducted in violation of the fundamental human rights of the subjects. This conclusion is based in part on the task force's assessment of these letters. Specifically, the task force found that

> [t]he researchers failed to satisfactorily inform the subjects and their families that the nutritional research studies were non-therapeutic; that is, that the research studies were never intended to benefit the human subjects as individuals but were intended to enhance the body of scientific knowledge concerning nutrition.

The letter in which consent from family members was requested, which was drafted by the former Fernald superintendent, failed to provide information that was reasonably necessary for an informed decision to be made.

Institutionalized Children Deserve Better Protection

The Fernald experiments also raise quite starkly the particular ethical difficulties associated with conducting research on members of institutionalized populations—especially where some of the residents have mental impairments. Living conditions in most of these institutions (including Fernald and Wrentham [Fernald's sister school]) have improved considerably in recent years, and sensitivity toward people with cognitive impairments has likewise increased. As Fred Boyce, a subject in one of these experiments has put it, "Fernald is a much better place today, and in no way does it operate like it did then. That's very important to know that."

"I won't tell you now about the severe physical and mental abuse, but I can assure you, it was no Boys' Town."

The Massachusetts Task Force describes conditions in state-operated facilities like Fernald, particularly as they bear on human experimentation, as follows:

Until the 1970s, the buildings were dirty and in disrepair, staff shortages were constant, brutality was often accepted, and programs were inadequate or nonexistent. There were no human rights committees or institutional review boards. If the Superintendent (in those days required to be a medical doctor) "cooperated" in an experiment and allowed residents to be subjects, few knew and no one protested. If nothing concerning the experiments appeared in the residents' medical records, if "request for consent" letters were less than forthright, or if no consent was obtained there was no one in a position of authority to halt or challenge such procedures.

Both researchers and policymakers appear to have been alert to considerations of harm and concerned about exposing children to an unacceptable level of risk.

Although public attitudes toward people who are institutionalized are admittedly different today than they were fifty years ago, it is likely that this state of affairs would have been troubling to most Americans even then. Historian Susan Lederer has revealed several episodes of experimentation with institutionalized children in America that caused considerable public outcry even before 1940, presaging the concern generated by Willowbrook when this research became a public issue in the 1960s. . . .

Pediatric researchers . . . agreed in principle that the convenience of conducting research on institutionalized children did not outweigh the moral problems associated with this practice:

Several investigators spoke about the practical advantages of using institutionalized children who are already assembled in one location and living within a standard, controlled environment. But the conferees agreed that there should be no differential recruitment of ward patients rather than private patients, of institutionalized children rather than children living in private homes, or of handicapped rather than healthy children.

The Boys Were Manipulated with Treats

A particularly poignant dimension of the unfairness of using institutionalized children as subjects of research is that it permits investigators to secure cooperation by offering as special treats what other, noninstitutionalized children would find far less exceptional. The extra attention of a "science club," a quart of milk, and an occasional outing were for the boys at

Fernald extraordinary opportunities. As Mr. Boyce put it:

> I won't tell you now about the severe physical and
> mental abuse, but I can assure you, it was no Boys'
> Town. The idea of getting consent for experiments un-
> der these conditions was not only cruel but hypocriti-
> cal. They bribed us by offering us special privileges,
> knowing that we had so little that we would do practi-
> cally anything for attention; and to say, I quote, "This
> is their debt to society," end quote, as if we were worth
> no more than laboratory mice, is unforgivable.

Even when a child was able to resist the offers of special
attention and refused to participate in the experiment, the
investigators seem to have been unwilling to respect the
child's decision. One MIT [Massachusetts Institute of Tech-
nology] researcher, Robert S. Harris, explicitly noted that
"it seemed to [him] that the three subjects who objected to
being included in the study [could] be induced to change
their minds." Harris believed that the recalcitrant children
could be "induced" to join in the study by emphasizing "the
Fernald Science Club angle of our work."

---

*The experiments at Fernald and at the
Wrentham School unfairly burdened children
who were already disadvantaged.*

From the perspective of the science, it was considered
important to conduct the research in an environment in
which the diet of the children-subjects could be easily controlled. From this standpoint, the institutional setting of
Fernald was ideal. The institutional settings of the boarding
schools in the Boston area, however, would have offered
much the same opportunity. Although the risks were small,
the "children of the elite" were rarely if ever selected for
such research. It is not likely that these children would have
been willing to submit to blood tests for extra milk or the
chance to go to the beach.

The question of what is ethical in the context of unfair
background conditions is always difficult. Perhaps the investigators, who were not responsible for the poor conditions at Fernald, believed that the opportunities provided to

the members of the Science Club brightened the lives of these children, if only briefly. Reasoning of this sort, however, can all too easily lead to unjustifiable disregard of the equal worth of all people and to unfair treatment.

Today [February 1995], fifty years after the Fernald experiments, still no federal regulations protecting institutionalized children from unfair treatment in research involving human subjects. The Committee strongly urges the federal government to fill this policy void by providing additional protections for institutionalized children.

The Children Did Face Minimal Risks

If an ethical evaluation of human experiments depended solely upon an assessment of the risks to subjects as they could reasonably be anticipated at the time, the radiation experiments conducted on children reviewed in this [article] would be relatively unproblematic. During this time, the association between radiation exposure and the subsequent development of cancer was not well understood, and in particular, little was known about iodine 131 [another substance administered to the children] and the risk of thyroid cancer. Both researchers and policymakers appear to have been alert to considerations of harm and concerned about exposing children to an unacceptable level of risk.

At the same time, however, the scientific community's experience with radionuclides [radioactive nuclides] in humans was limited, and this approach to medical investigation was new. Although the available data about human risk were encouraging and the biological susceptibility of children to the effects of radiation was not appreciated, we are left with the lingering question of whether investigators and agency officials were *sufficiently* cautious as they began their work with children. This is a difficult judgment to make at any point in the development of a field of human research; it is particularly difficult to make at forty or fifty years' remove. Investigators and officials had to make decisions under conditions of considerable uncertainty; this is commonplace in science and in medicine. Although the biological susceptibility of children was not then known, investigators and officials held the view that children should be accorded extra protection in the conduct of human research, and they made what they thought were appropriate adjustments when using children as subjects. If human research never proceeded in the face of uncertainty, there would be no such experiments. How little uncertainty is acceptable in research involving children is a question that remains unresolved. Today, we continue to debate what constitutes minimal risk to children, in radiation and in other areas of research. The regulations governing research on children offer little in the way of guidance, either with respect to conditions of uncertainty about risk or when risks are known.

As best as we can determine, in eleven of the twenty-one experiments we reviewed, the risks were in a range that would today likely be considered as more than minimal, and thus as unacceptable in nontherapeutic research with children according to current federal regulations. It is possible, however, that four of the eleven might be considered acceptable by the "minor increase over minimal risk" standard. In these four experiments, the average risk estimates were between one and two per thousand, the studies were directed at the subjects' medical conditions, and they may well have had the potential to obtain information of "vital importance.". . .

The Boys Were Treated as Second-Class Citizens

The experiments at Fernald and at the Wrentham School unfairly burdened children who were already disadvantaged, children whose interests were less well protected than those children living with their parents or children who were socially privileged. At the Fernald School, where more is known, there was some attempt to solicit the permission of parents, but the information provided was incomplete and misleading. The investigators successfully secured the cooperation of the children with offers of extra milk and an occasional outing—incentives that would not likely have induced children who were less starved for attention to willingly submit to repeated blood tests.

One researcher speaking almost thirty-five years ago set out the fundamental moral issue with particular frankness and clarity:

> . . . we are talking here about first and second class citizens. This is a concept none of our consciences will allow us to live with. . . . The thing we must all avoid is two types of citizenry.

It might have been common for researchers to take advantage of the convenience of experimenting on institutionalized children, but the Committee does not believe that convenience offsets the moral problems associated with employing these vulnerable children as research subjects—now or decades ago.

3

The Federal Government Ignored Reports About the Fernald Study

Edward J. Markey

In 1994, after the *Boston Globe* broke the story about the radiation experiments at the Fernald school, several Massachusetts state agencies assembled a task force to investigate the matter. The resulting report found that although the doses of radioactive calcium fed to the boys were unlikely to cause them any long-term health damage, the experiments should never have taken place. In the following letter addressed to task force chairperson Frederick M. Misilo Jr., Massachusetts senator Edward J. Markey commends state officials and agencies for their rapid response to the news of the experiments. On the other hand, he also expresses concern that the U.S. Department of Energy had concealed its knowledge of the Fernald study when the House Subcommittee on Energy Conservation and Power requested information about radiation studies in the 1980s. This secrecy on the part of the federal government leads Markey to question how many other populations of institutionalized children have been the victims of similar experiments.

March 4, 1994
Dear Chairperson Misilo:
    It has been my privilege to be involved with the Task Force [to Review Human Subject Research], and I am hon-

Edward J. Markey, "Letter to Frederick M. Misilo Jr.," *Report on the Use of Radioactive Materials in Human Subject Research That Involved Residents of State Operated Facilities Within the Commonwealth of Massachusetts from 1943 through 1973*, edited by the Task Force on Human Subject Research, March 1994.

ored by your request for my comments on the occasion of the Task Force Report. I am pleased to inform you that the response of officials and institutions in Massachusetts to the experiments at the Fernald School stands in stark contrast to the past response at the federal level in regard to experiments with ionizing radiation and human subjects. While it has taken years to prompt an adequate response at the federal level, the response in Massachusetts was vigorous from the outset, with the goals of full disclosure and rectification of past events. . . .

The Subcommittee staff report was essentially ignored by the Reagan administration, and it was left to gather dust on a shelf.

As you know, in October 1986, I released a staff report of the House Subcommittee on Energy Conservation and Power, which described experiments with human subjects and ionizing radiation that provided little or no medical benefit to those exposed. This report was based on documents requested from the Department of Energy, related to experiments funded by its predecessor agencies. The staff report recommended medical follow-up of the subjects of these experiments, and recommended that experiments of the type described, which apparently ended in the early 1970's, never be conducted again.

An Appendix to the 1986 report described current federal regulations on human experimentation, including four general principles:

- Risks to subjects should be minimized;
- Risks to subjects should be reasonable in relation to anticipated benefits, and the importance of the knowledge that may reasonably be expected to result;
- Subjects should be selected in an equitable manner; and
- Informed consent shall be sought from each prospective subject or authorized representative.

Informed consent includes a clear description of the risks and benefits of the experimental procedure.

Additional restrictions are in effect for experiments with children, and such experiments generally require a benefit for the subject or a benefit for the health of children generally.

The Subcommittee staff report was essentially ignored by the [Ronald] Reagan administration, and it was left to gather dust on a shelf until Secretary of Energy Hazel O'Leary accepted its findings late in 1993. Secretary O'Leary and the [Bill] Clinton administration through its Human Radiation Interagency Working Group, are committed to full disclosure of experiments with ionizing radiation and human subjects, while protecting the privacy of subjects and their families, and to medical follow-up where it is feasible and indicated. Although it has taken a long time for action at the federal level, I have been gratified by the leadership of the Clinton administration on this issue.

Late in 1993, information was released on the Fernald School experiments, where schoolboys were fed radioactive iron or calcium in their breakfast meals in the 1940s and 1950s. These experiments violated at least two of the present standards for using human subjects: The children at the school represented a segment of society that deserved protection, not exploitation; and their parents were deceived about the nature of the experiments when they gave their consent for participation. . . .

Responsible Parties Admitted Guilt

In contrast to the experience at the federal level, officials of the Massachusetts Department of Mental Retardation [DMR] from the outset registered profound shock and dismay over the experiments. The DMR has shown no interest in defending mistakes committed in the past. The formation of the Task Force and the investigation by its staff have been designed to provide full disclosure of the extent of human experimentation with ionizing radiation at all DMR facilities.

I have also been impressed with the response of Massachusetts academic institutions, whose affiliated scientists conducted the experiments of the 1940s, 50s, and 60s. Dr. Charles Vest, present president of MIT, acknowledged that while doses at the Fernald School may have been relatively low, he was "sorry" for the experiments, because of the children selected and the lack of informed consent. MIT explained that President Vest issued his statement because "it seemed the decent thing to do," and I applaud his decency. Likewise, the efforts of present officials and scientists at

Harvard University brought to the attention of the Task Force experiments in the 1960s at the Wrentham School, where tiny children were fed non-radioactive iodide and radioactive iodine-131, to test a possible "countermeasure" to fallout from atomic bombs. Present leaders of academic institutions have been interested in full disclosure, not in defending mistakes of the past.

Expanded Investigation

The revelation of these experiments at Massachusetts institutions has raised my concern over whether the full extent of testing nationally has been identified. The experiments at the Fernald School were funded in part by the National Institutes of Health and the Atomic Energy Commission, and should have been reported to my Subcommittee in response to its requests in the 1980s. The scientific paper reporting the Wrentham School experiments noted that the test subjects were chosen "because it was desirable to secure children living under constant conditions of environment, diet, and iodide uptake," and similar considerations contributed to selection of students at the Fernald School as experimental subjects. These revelations cause concern about whether institutionalized populations presented too great a temptation for experimental investigators across the country.

Accordingly, I have written to Secretary of Health and Human Services Donna Shalala, whose department is reviewing its files as part of the federal Interagency Working Group. I have requested that in its review, her Department give heightened attention to experiments on the developmentally challenged. The experiments at the Wrentham School were funded by the U.S. Public Health Service, Division of Radiological Health, and I have also requested special attention to the files of that office, to determine if other questionable experiments were conducted in the name of understanding exposures from atomic fallout.

I recognize that because of the limits of time, the Task Force report is focused on experiments with ionizing radiation. I also recognize and commend your determination in the future to examine exposures to other agents at DMR facilities. The Task Force efforts thus represents a prototype that can be replicated across the country in at least two regards: Firstly, this is to my knowledge the first systematic governmental investigation of experiments with ionizing radiation and institutionalized subjects. Secondly, the DMR has recognized that it is appropriate to investigate experimental exposures to dangerous chemical and biological agents in addition to radiation. I have already recommended expanding the efforts at the federal level to identify experiments with such additional hazardous agents.

Once again, I commend your leadership, and I appreciate the opportunity to be associated with this admirable effort. I offer whatever assistance would be appropriate in implementing the recommendations of the Task Force, and I would welcome the chance to continue assisting your investigations at the DMR.

Sincerely,
Edward J. Markey
Member of Congress

4

A Fernald Researcher Defends the Experiments on Children

Constantine J. Maletskos, interviewed
by Darrell Fisher and Karoline Gourley

Under Department of Energy secretary Hazel O'Leary's direction, the Advisory Committee on Human Radiation Experiments produced an oral history project of various radiation experiments, including interviews with researchers involved in some of the experiments. In the following 1995 interview with physicist Constantine J. Maletskos, physicist Darrell Fisher and government researcher Karoline Gourley ask him about the Fernald school experiments he helped to conduct. Maletskos maintains that the experiments were extremely safe and that they yielded valuable information about nutrition that would have been impossible to gain otherwise. He also adds that being allowed to participate in the radiation experiments brightened the boys' otherwise bleak lives.

---

*D**arrell Fisher* . . . You were also involved in some controversial studies in the early '50s on calcium metabolism and uptake in man; was this using calcium-45 [radioactive form of calcium] produced at the [MIT] cyclotron [particle accelerator], or was this calcium obtained somewhere else?

Constantine Maletskos Let's make sure about the use of the word "controversial." They weren't *controversial* at the time they were done; they became controversial in 1993, [when

Constantine J. Maletskos, interviewed by Darrell Fisher and Karoline Gourley, "Oral History of the Health Physicist Constantine J. Maletskos, PhD," *Oral Histories: Department of Energy Openness: Human Radiation Experiments: Roadmap to the Project*, January 20, 1995.

Secretary of Energy O'Leary launched her openness campaign to "come clean" about the alleged abuses of the past].

Fisher That's what I meant.

Maletskos I had mentioned that before I got [to] the Radioactivity Center in 1948, an experiment had been done by the [Massachusetts Institute of Technology] [MIT] Department of Nutrition on the absorption effects of phytates[1] on radioactive iron because radioactive iron was available; [it had been used] for the blood preservation studies.

Here was a situation where we wanted to know what phytates do to [iron absorption] because we're sweating out [a problem]; the world eats cereals left and right, especially the people who aren't very well-off [financially], and especially now in what we now call developing countries, and it could be a serious [malnutrition problem] if you're just holding the iron away if they happen to eat the wrong "cereal.". . .

The kids that I saw that had been chosen [for the experiment] looked fine to me.

Fisher Can you describe this experiment?

Maletskos Well, I wasn't there, [but] I can describe now what the next step was, which is: later on, the same problem would occur with calcium, so calcium and phytates became an important thing to study.

When I came to the Radioactivity Center, this experiment had already been conceived and designed, and was waiting for animal experiments to be done. [These animal experiments] were being done at MIT because [we] didn't know what the dosimetry [measurement of dose of radioactivity] was going to be like [on humans] and how much you could give that would [be] consider[ed] safe.

Nobody had ever done a calcium experiment before using radioactive calcium, calcium-45, which you could now get from the U.S. Atomic Energy Commission program; so all the initial work that was developed ([namely,] use of the students from the mental institution, any informed consent, the general design of the experiment; not the details, because that would come when you knew everything) had already been decided upon. So I was not involved in any of

---

1. natural ingredients in grains thought to interfere with iron absorption in the body

that part of it. I was involved in the dosimetry, the development of techniques for making the measurements and how to analyze the data eventually, and all this kind of stuff.

Fisher These are important aspects of dosimetry; but do you remember how the subjects were chosen by the physicians?

Researcher Found Conditions Appalling

Maletskos I do know, because I was involved; there were criteria set for what the status of the subjects had to be. Obviously, you couldn't have a subject that was sick from something that had to do with the alimentary tract [the canal from mouth to anus]. Is that what you are referring to? All of those considerations were all in there: how you chose which subject actually became a part of the group that was going to be in the experimental group had a lot to do [with them]; how easy it was for that [decision] to be managed; and was the subject willing and not afraid of the experiment—that sort of thing.

They were essentially young kids, you see; I saw those kids eventually, when I was invited to one of the Christmas dinners. This is what they called the Science Club Group, and it's been misinterpreted from the very beginning; I can't believe it! They were very nice young kids. My first reaction was, [when] I'd [visited] the mental institution in the earlier phases of it, and boy there were some sights in there that still bother me today.

Karoline Gourley Like what?

Maletskos Well, the kind of physical situation some of the people, some of them were plain skeletons, they couldn't move and everything else; it was really difficult to see, you'd see one person and you'd feel sorry for [him], [but when] you [would] see a lot of them[, it was very difficult].

[But with regard to the boys in the experiment,] there was nothing wrong with them. These were people that had to be in an institution like that and they were being cared for well, as far as I could see; the beds were cleaned, there were no smells around, at least in the places that I had gone to. So as far as I was concerned that place was being run very well; now what was going on in detail, I don't know, and I don't know how they were chosen. But the kids that I saw that had been chosen [for the experiment] looked fine to me and essentially looked normal to me. It turns out that a lot of them *were* normal; they were just put in there because the[ir] families couldn't handle them.

Fisher Were they considered a part of the Science Club because they had participated in the experiment?

Enticements Meant to Encourage Boys

Maletskos It sounded to me like an afterthought; it *wasn't* originally set up as an enticing method; and remember, even today, there are ads in the paper inviting you to participate and stipends [payments for participation] [are indicated], and I've seen one stipend that goes up to 3,000 dollars. Is that enticement or is that not enticement? The object is that you've got to pay this person for their time. But you don't want to overpay the person, to make sure that you [are not] forcing them, in effect, to come off the street [to jump at a rare chance to earn good money].

The [children] were picked—and it was an afterthought, as I gather—that somebody was talking about: "It would be nice [to do something for them because] these kids have been involved, we've had to jab them [with needles], and they had to eat a meal—every little drop of it, because you wanted to be sure they got 100 percent of the radioactivity—wouldn't it be nice to do something for them?" So to make them feel like they were special, they called it the Science Group, and the only thing they got was one meal, maybe twice in their whole career, outside of the institution at the MIT Faculty Club and as I remember, and they got a [small] present.

As far as I could see, things looked like they were being handled well.

Fisher So this was done at the MIT Faculty Club?

Maletskos Yes, because it was easier to bring them there; you could control them and all this sort of thing.

Fisher Did the parents receive any stipend?

Maletskos No, there was no stipend in money; the meal was the stipend, and a little-baby gift [(i.e., a gift of small value)].

Fisher You mentioned the payment of money for participation.

Maletskos I mentioned that relative to current times; it

had nothing to do with money back in those days. I was using the illustration [that] if you wanted to call this enticement, it's just as enticing these days when you have a stipend. You've got to remember that there are a lot of things that are going [on today] that are identical, only we think they're okay now.

Fisher Did the parents bring them to the [Radioactivity] Center or did the hospital [provide transportation]?

Maletskos They had already been brought there; they were already residents of the Fernald School.

MIT's Involvement

Gourley How did MIT hook up with Fernald?

Maletskos I don't know; could have been a happenstance situation, for all I know, but I don't know. I literally do not know. It must have been done by [MIT] Professor [Bob] Harris that I mentioned already, and some contact who knew about the school, and then he eventually contact[ed] the superintendent of the school. There was no way for the school to know that MIT wanted to do this.

Fisher Do you remember if the parents were involved in this study?

Maletskos I don't know anything about that. All I know is what's been found out since then, and we can talk about that later on if you want. Anyway, as far as I could see, things looked like they were being handled well. Again, remember what I said earlier, the school was responsible for getting their subjects, and it was up to them to do that properly, it was up to MIT on its part to do everything properly in terms of the radioactivity and the handling [of] the venous puncturing and [associated sampling].

The Radioactivity Center's involvement was making sure they got the right amount of [radio]activity, which essentially fell into my lap, and that we had done the dosimetry correctly and everything else [related to measurements]. Remember, I mentioned there were animal studies going on. Well, those went on two years before [Maletskos's fellow researcher, Robley] Evans would give an okay to do this [experiment]. That just shows you how much care was involved in those days. Here the Department of Nutrition [at MIT] was champing at the bit to want to do the experiment and Felix Bronner, who was going in to do his Ph.D. on this subject, was champing because he didn't want to stay there [in grad school] forever. And Evans [was] saying, "We [have to learn about the research for] a couple of years before we can make any decisions about how much [of the radioactive substance] we're going to give them [(the human subjects)]." Because [back then,] you didn't know anything about what the metabolism [of calcium] was.

Who Benefited from Study Results?

Gourley Was it, at the time, considered a metabolism experiment or a dietary experiment?

Maletskos No, it was a *dietary* experiment as far as the children were concerned; the animals were rats: *that* was just an animal experiment. This was a dietary experiment on those subjects who are likely to get in trouble because they were growing kids [who drank] a lot of milk and [ate] a lot of cereal. Even at the institution they were getting a lot of cereals because it was a cheap food, but it was a nutritious food.

If you want to look at it from a broad scope, it was a benefit to them to know this [(about the calcium and iron uptake)]. It was [a] benefit to the whole world to know it because the whole world eats cereals.

It was a dietary *experiment as far as the children were concerned.*

Gourley How did the funding come in for this?

Maletskos The funding [for] the Radioactivity Center was [from the] Atomic Energy Commission [AEC] at the time and there was Office of Naval Research [funding as well], but I assume the bulk of it was from the AEC. (I assume I wasn't there watching the balance books as to how much money was [being] taken out of each pocket.) The other side was Quaker Oats [the cereal company], which was supporting the [nutrition] research, mainly the stipend for the graduate students and a few chemicals [reagents (substances used to initiate biological activity)] and that sort of thing; the institution [(the Fernald School)] was supporting it in the sense that they were housing the [children] and taking care of them.

Gourley I was looking through some of the papers over at the Center, and in Robley Evans's personal collection and I noticed some letters—

Maletskos Where was this personal collection—you mean those bound books?

Gourley The Robley Evans collection at MIT Archives.

Maletskos That's the set that I have over here, I assume.

Gourley I noticed that there was some correspondence and that sort of thing with the [United Nations] World Health Organization. Were *they* particularly interested in the results?

Radiation Studies Streamlined Research

Maletskos I don't know, because I don't recall any of that; I have no recollection about that, even if I did know [at that time]. But I'm sure, he [(Evans)] was involved in an awful lot of things because this Radioactivity Center was one of the sources of development of this whole field [of radiation measurements and application of isotopes in medicine and biology]. You have to keep in mind, keep it in perspective, [that] this was a real challenging era that people looked forward to as being a way to learn a lot of things that you were dying to learn but couldn't do it because there was no way to [do the research].

Gourley Could you just name some of those things "Joe Q Public" wanted to learn that radiation experiments helped them learn?

Maletskos They were doing absorption experiments; nobody wants to listen on how you used to do an absorption experiment [and] I'm not going to take a long time to do that experiment; it took one week.

To do that experiment the old-fashion way, you had to find your people [in] the same fashion and everything else, put them on a fixed diet that would essentially make them normal, hold them on that diet and measure every day—or not every day, but frequently enough for weeks and weeks and weeks—until they became stabilized. [And then you had to] give them another diet and do the same thing again for weeks and weeks and weeks; and there [would be] variations in the answers of both of them; and unless there was a big change, you didn't know what happened. In the meantime, you were collecting blood and excreta [body waste] and you were doing chemical analysis on excreta until you were going blind.

Fisher What types of samples did you measure?

Maletskos We measured feces, urine, and blood; and, of

course, the original material and the aliquot [measurement for chemical analysis] that actually became part of [the administered radioactivity].

Fisher Over what length of time were the calcium-45 nutrition studies [conducted]?

Tiny Doses Were Carefully Administered

Maletskos It would be a week's worth of collection—that's *it*. By then, we were giving so little [radioactivity]—now remember, the doses turned out—(I don't remember what the calculations are that I made, but when this whole "scandal" started in December of 199[3], I made a quick back-of-the-envelope calculation and I [came up with], like, 10 or 20 millirem [one-thousandth of a rem, a standard dosage of radiation]). It turns out the average was ten millirem.

Back in [the] early 1950s, we had good detection sensitivity, so that we could do an experiment and on those young kids give no more than ten millirem; pretty doggone good fundamental radioactivity physics and instrumentation. You can't do any better now, [though] you might do better with calcium-47.

5

Former Radiation Victims Are Bothered by Memories of the Fernald Experiments

Richard Higgins

After conducting interviews with former members of the Fernald school science club, *Boston Globe* journalist Richard Higgins wrote the following exposé on the abuse the boys involved in the radiation experiments suffered. As Higgins describes, neither the small rewards offered them as boys nor the monetary compensation won as a result of a class action lawsuit filed on their behalf could erase the men's memories of the institution and the embarrassment and shame of having been taken advantage of by adults who were supposed to have protected and cared for them. Official findings that the experiments did them "no real harm" only added to the pain and anger they felt.

In 1952, after his parents sent him to live at the Walter E. Fernald State School, Joe Almeida was recruited by its "science club." To the 10-year-old boy, it looked like a good deal. Members got a "special beneficial diet," including extra milk, plus trips to the beach and baseball park.

The only problem is that Almeida and as many as 88 other Fernald residents were the experiment. The Massachusetts Institute of Technology [MIT] and Quaker Oats, with approval from state officials and the Atomic Energy Com-

Richard Higgins, "Haunted by the 'Science Club' Monetary Offer Can't Erase His Memory," *Boston Globe*, January 18, 1998. Copyright © 1998 by the Globe Newspaper Company. Reproduced by permission of Copyright Clearance Center, Inc.

mission, secretly fed them radiation-spiked oatmeal and milk. Today [1998], Almeida is the only survivor of the experiments who remains connected to the school. He has worked in the garage since 1984. Although he said that the Fernald School of today is a "completely different place" than the one he attended, and that he does not blame his current employer, there are moments when anger rises up in him.

"I do get mad sometimes when I think about it," Almeida said last week in the kitchen of his Waltham [Massachusetts] apartment. "They were supposed to be protecting us, and here they were feeding us this stuff without our knowledge or consent."

Suit Brings the Truth to Light

Late last month [December 1997], MIT and the Chicago cereal maker, while denying any wrongdoing, agreed to settle a class-action suit filed by Almeida and 14 former Fernald residents, offering them $1.85 million. A hearing will be held in early April to determine if all sides agree to the settlement.

Since the suit was filed in 1995, others who belonged to the so-called science club have been identified. Lawyers for the plaintiffs say that they now know of about 25 certified participants in the radiation experiments. Many of them, including Almeida, were wards of the state who were inaccurately classified as mentally retarded.

MIT concedes that the testing took place in the late 1940s and 1950s and has apologized for it. But the university maintains that the boys were not harmed because they were exposed to "minute" amounts of radiation, levels about equal to the natural background radiation in the environment.

Since the suit was filed in 1995, others who belonged to the so-called science club have been identified.

Quaker has said that it provided only a "small grant" to pay for the experiment, the purpose of which was to see if the nutrients in Quaker oatmeal, in particular calcium and iron, travel throughout the body. (Radioactive nutrients made it possible to track the digested oatmeal.) The company wanted to match the advertising claims of its competitor, Cream of Wheat, which contains farina.

For Almeida, who is now 55, memory of the science club is tinged with his memory of his years at Fernald, which began in 1951 and ended when he ran away in 1960. During that time, Almeida said that he was confined, forced to do manual labor, frequently beaten, and sexually abused.

For that reason, he said, any monetary settlement would necessarily fall short. "They took my childhood, my innocence away from me, so how can they ever pay me back?" he asked. "As far as I am concerned, they couldn't give me enough money. I can never get back what I really want because it's gone."

Almeida joined the class-action suit as "John Doe" and has not previously spoken for attribution. However, Almeida, along with Fred Boyce of Norwell [Massachusetts], has been one of the unofficial leaders in the plaintiff group.

Food Experiments Were Part of an Enforced Routine

The food experiments by the MIT nutritional lab began in 1946 and continued for about a decade.

According to the suit the plaintiffs filed in federal district court, the children were tricked because they were told that they were going to be part of a science club. There was, in fact, no science, but there were special privileges, including a Christmas party on Memorial Drive and trips to Revere Beach and Fenway Park [in Boston].

Almeida, who said that being a part of the group was viewed by the residents as desirable, said he recalls being given a Hopalong Cassidy [children's TV character] mug.

For their part, the boys had to eat together in a specially designated area, give frequent blood and urine samples, and take whatever pills they were given, often twice a day, according to Almeida. He says he recalls a "big brown jar" of pills and drinking some "clear liquid stuff in a paper cup once in the morning for one year."

"We didn't think anything of it because it was routine to do what you were told," Almeida said. "We didn't have any freedom." Those who ran the school "had total control, and they put the fear of God in you if you didn't behave."

He described having to sit on settees, or benches, his arms folded, for a part of each day under orders to not speak to other boys or to attendants. "If you got caught talking, they'd hit you with a wooden hanger, and I mean they'd really wail at you," he said. He added that he was also forced to swallow a bite of yellow soap with a tablespoon of cod liver oil.

Were the Experiments Safe?

One question that haunts Almeida and other participants is just how much radiation was used in the tests. In 1994, a state panel, while acknowledging that the boys' civil rights had been violated, found that small amounts of radioactive calcium and iron known to have been ingested by at least 74 Fernald residents had no discernible effects on their health.

The class-action suit alleges, however, that of the 3,000 doses of radioactive material that were authorized for the food experiment, only 150 doses have been accounted for.

"It infuriates me when they say that there was no damage," said Boyce, of Norwell, noting that scientific views vary on the effects of low-level radiation, and that records of most of the radioactive material are missing, allowing for the possibility that exposure rates were higher.

It infuriates me when they say that there was no damage.

In the end, amounts are not the issue, according to Michael K. Mattchen, an attorney with Dangel, Donlan and Fine, the firm representing the plaintiffs. "These experiments upon young, institutionalized boys are indefensible," he said. "The betrayal inherent in using them as human guinea pigs violates every concept of civil and human rights."

Experiments Were Part of Larger Abuse

Almeida said that the oatmeal experiment is just the most dramatic of numerous medical and nutritional experiments conducted on boys and girls at Fernald without their informed consent. Other tests involved high blood pressure and birth control pills, he said. He said he remembers having to ingest the pills in front of attendants to make sure he didn't spit them out.

Almeida said he was sent to the Fernald School in 1951 by probation officers in East Cambridge [Massachusetts], where he lived, because he had run away from his home many times. Almeida said that he ran away because his stepmother beat him.

At the time, he said, the sign at the main entrance said, "Walter E. Fernald School, Home for the Feeble-Minded."

"There were a lot of kids who were retarded, but there were also a lot who were not," he said. Those who were not included children who had become wards of the state and were dumped at the school, according to Mattchen, the lawyer.

Boyce, who also belonged to the science club, said that there are other living participants who don't want to come forward because of the stigma of having been at Fernald.

"I know of some who have not even told their own family that they were there," he said.

That same stigma influenced Almeida's decision to return to Fernald in 1984 as an employee. Because Fernald was the only school he had ever attended, he said he was frequently denied employment and had to settle for what he could get.

The job he gained at the school in 1984 made him a state employee, offering him what he said were the best pay and benefits he had received. Almeida is also a poet who has written about his experiences at the school.

"It was definitely hard at first, and there were times when I cried or just felt like leaving," he said. "But I also knew the place." And Fernald had changed.

"I don't look at it as the same place that I was at," Almeida said.

When he resolved to stay, he said, he did so with a promise: "I knew that if I saw any abuse, I'd be the first one to snitch."

6

Cold War Fears Spurred the Unethical Radiation Experiments at Fernald

Tom Mashberg

In the following editorial, journalist Tom Mashberg argues that the researchers in the Fernald school radiation experiment easily rationalized their actions because of the Cold War fervor that had seized the country. In the race to gain more information about radiation and nuclear power to beat their Communist enemies, the United States subjected many groups of unsuspecting citizens to unethical testing. In the 1950s it was considered unpatriotic to question the government, and as a result, the most vulnerable members of society, including the mentally retarded children at Fernald school, became guinea pigs in dangerous experiments. Mashberg is an editor at the Boston Herald.

I t was the era of "duck and cover," when schoolchildren slipped under rickety wooden desks during mock nuclear alerts. It was a time when Army men were ordered to march toward the epicenter of an atomic test blast, and did so without question. It was a day when radiation seemed like a great new toy, and scientists driven to understand its properties handled globes of radioactive plutonium with screwdrivers and rubber gloves.

It was the first decade of the Atomic Age, and the start of the Cold War. A time when a US government swollen

Tom Mashberg, "When Radiation Drew No Fear," *Boston Globe*, January 2, 1994. Copyright © 1994 by the Globe Newspaper Company. Reproduced by permission of Copyright Clearance Center, Inc.

But even now there are experts who warn that the use of radiation today is a scandal that will be uncovered four decades down the road.

"These revelations, shocking as they seem, are in no way atypical today," said Dr. Samuel Epstein, an epidemiologist at the University of Illinois who has has written many articles questioning the current uses of radiation in mammograms and other procedures. "I think we're still seeing misconduct in this field, and manipulation of the data. Maybe now that the spotlight is shining we can look at this in the proper way."

Still, the ethical guidelines in place today would dissuade much of the arrogance condoned four decades ago.

"I'm not lightly shocked by what happened in the 1950s," said Halberstam. "But this shocks me. I mean, I lived through that era and it could be horrible. You were supposed to buy your own bomb shelter, for god's sake.

"But a government does not have the right to abuse its most vulnerable—the mentally retarded! You don't experiment with people in this country. That's what it's all about."

For Further Research

Books

Christian Bernadac, *Devil's Doctors: Medical Experiments on Human Subjects in the Concentration Camps*. Geneva: Ferni, 1978.

Allan M. Brandt, *No Magic Bullet*. New York: Oxford University Press, 1987.

Kenneth Getz and Deborah Borfitz, *Informed Consent: A Guide to the Risks and Benefits of Volunteering for Clinical Trials*. Boston: Thomson/CenterWatch, 2003.

Andrew Goliszek, *In the Name of Science: A History of Secret Programs, Medical Research, and Human Experimentation*. New York: St. Martin's, 2003.

Fred Gray, *Bus Ride to Justice: Changing the System by the System: The Life and Works of Fred D. Gray, Preacher, Attorney, Politician*. Montgomery, AL: Black Belt, 1995.

James H. Jones, *Bad Blood: The Tuskegee Syphilis Experiment: New and Expanded Edition*. New York: Free Press, 1993.

Martin R. Lipp, *Respectful Treatment—the Human Side of Medical Care*. Hagerstown, MD: Medical Department, Harper & Row, 1977.

Massachusetts Department of Mental Retardation, *Report on the Use of Radioactive Materials in Human Research Involving Residents of the State Operated Facilities of the Commonwealth of Massachusetts from 1943–1973*. Boston: Massachusetts Department of Mental Retardation, 1993.

David McBride, *From TB to AIDS: Epidemics Among Urban Blacks Since 1900*. Albany: State University of New York Press, 1991.

Sheila McLean, *Old Law, New Medicine: Medical Ethics and Human Rights*. London: Pandora, 1999.

Jonathan D. Moreno, *Undue Risk*. New York: W.H. Freeman, 1999.

Susan Quinn, *Human Trials: Scientists, Investors, and Patients in the Quest for a Cure.* Cambridge, MA: Perseus, 2001.

Eileen Welsome, *The Plutonium Files: America's Secret Medical Experiments in the Cold War.* New York: Dial, 1999.

Periodicals

Scott Allen, "Radiation Used on Retarded Postwar Experiments Done at Fernald School," *Boston Globe*, December 26, 1993.

Boston Globe, "U.S. Apologizes to Thousands It Exposed to Radiation," October 4, 1995.

Michael D'Antonio, "Atomic Guinea Pigs," *New York Times Magazine*, August 31, 1997.

Michael M. Davis, "The Ability of Patients to Pay for Treatment of Syphilis," *Journal of Social Hygiene*, October 1932.

Ebony, "Condemned to Die for Science," November 1972.

Amy Fairchild and Ronald Bayer, "Uses and Abuses of Tuskegee," *Science*, May 7, 1999.

Federal Register, "The Belmont Report: Ethical Principles and Guidelines for the Protection of Human Subjects," doc. 79-12065, April 18, 1979.

Saul Krugman and Joan P. Giles, "Viral Hepatitis: New Light on an Old Disease," *Journal of the American Medical Association*, no. 212, 1970.

Saul Krugman et al., "Infectious Hepatitis: Studies of Its Natural History and Prevention," *New England Journal of Medicine*, no. 258, 1958.

Lancet, "Australia Antigen and Hepatitis," March 6, 1971.

———, "More About Australia Antigen and Hepatitis," August 15, 1970.

Susan Lederer, "The Tuskegee Syphilis Study in the Context of American Medical Research," *Sigerist Circle Newsletter and Bibliography*, Winter 1994.

Modern Medicine, "How Much for the Patient, How Much for Medical Science?: An Interview with Saul Krugman," no. 30, 1974.

New York Times, "Interview with Saul Krugman," April 18, 1972.

Pasqual J. Pesare et al., "Untreated Syphilis in the Male Negro," *Journal of Venereal Disease Information*, no. 27, 1946.

Physics Today, "Clinton Apologizes for Cold War Experiments," November 1995.

Lynda Richardson, "Experiment Leaves Legacy of Distrust of New AIDS Drugs," *New York Times*, April 21, 1997.

Eunice Rivers et al., "Twenty Years of Follow-Up Experience in a Long-Range Medical Study," *Public Health Reports*, no. 68, 1953.

Donald H. Rockwell et al., "The Tuskegee Study of Untreated Syphilis," *Archives of Internal Medicine*, no. 114, 1961.

David Rothman, "Were Tuskegee and Willowbrook Studies in Nature?" *Hastings Center Report*, vol. 12, no. 2, 1982.

Carol Kaesuk Yoon, "Families Emerge as Silent Victims of Tuskegee Syphilis Experiments," *New York Times*, May 12, 1997.

Video

Miss Evers' Boys, New York: HBO Home Video, 1997.

Web Sites

Archives & Special Collections—Guide to Willowbrook Resources, www.library.csi.cuny.edu/archives/Willowbrook RG.htm. This Web site provides a background of the Willowbrook school as well as a discussion of the now infamous Willowbrook hepatitis study performed there.

Resources on Nonconsensual Human Experimentation, http://gpc.edu/~shale/humanities/composition/assignments/experiment.html. Put together for a class on human experimentation by Steven Hale, associate professor of humanities at Perimeter College in Clarkston, Georgia, this site provides a wealth of information about human medical experiments.

Centers for Disease Control and Prevention: The Tuskegee Syphilis Study, www.cdc.gov/nchstp/od/tuskegee. This site provides an extensive, balanced source for information about the Tuskegee syphilis study and links to many related sites.

Index